S0-BRV-929

DATE DUE

MAY 2 4 2005		
JUN 7 2007		
GAYLORD		PRINTED IN U.S.A.

POST-MASTECTOMY

A personal guide to physical & emotional recovery

362
.196
W775p

POST-MASTECTOMY

t © 1976 by Win Ann Winkler. Copyright under International and Pan-
 Copyright Conventions. All rights reserved, including the right to reproduce this
portions thereof in any form, except for the inclusion of brief quotations in a
All inquiries should be addressed to Hawthorn Books, Inc., 260 Madison Avenue,
, New York 10016. This book was manufactured in the United States of America
ished simultaneously in Canada by Prentice-Hall of Canada, Limited, 1870
nt Road, Scarborough, Ontario.

f Congress Catalog Card Number: 75–28699

3015–5948–0

 6 7 8 9 10

Illinois Benedictine C
Theodore Lownik L
Lisle, Illinois

POST-MASTEC

A perso
to physical & e

by WIN A

Co
Ar
bo
re
N
ar
B

L

HAWTI

P

To Marion and Charlie

Contents

Foreword by Jerome A. Urban, M.D.   ix
Acknowledgments   xi
Introduction   xiii

Phase I: You've Won Half the Battle

1	The Mastectomy Mystique	3
2	First Steps in the Hospital	8
3	First Steps at Home	17
4	Anxiety and Depression	31
5	A Clearing in the Woods	38
6	Facts and Fiction	43
7	Facing Our Deepest Fears	49
8	Related Health Matters	53
9	Deeper than the Scar	58

Phase II: Reawakening

10	Taking the Bull by the Horns	67
11	Diet	72
12	All-Around Beauty Care	80
13	Exercise	88
14	Clothes	106
15	The Prosthesis	127
16	Sports and Physical Activity	136
17	Sex	141

Contents

18 *Family and Social Relationships*   147
19 *Cultivating Enlightened Selfishness*   156
20 *Vultures of the Living*   162
21 *Womanhood Awakened*   170

Afterword   173

Appendixes

A *Approved Cancer Detection Centers*   177
B *Comprehensive Cancer Centers*   181
C *Shopping Information*   185

Suggested Reading   189

Index   191

Foreword

As a practicing surgeon who has specialized in breast cancer for the past thirty years, I have seen the outlook for women afflicted by breast cancer change from one of despair to one of hope. Although it is still too early to quote long-term statistics, we can anticipate a markedly increased survival rate over that obtained ten and twenty years ago, largely due to improved diagnostic techniques.

Between 1955 and 1964, in our own experience, the overall ten-year survival rate for primary operable breast cancer was 57 percent following adequate treatment. In the case of *minimal cancer*, treatment by less than radical mastectomy (modified radical) resulted in a ten-year survival rate of 95 percent! At the opposite end of the spectrum, women who had passed the localized stage, whose malignancy had spread to the regional nodes, attained a 33 percent ten-year survival rate following *radical* mastectomy. When women in this category were treated by *extended radical mastectomy*, the ten-year survival rate jumped to 54 percent.

Obviously, with earlier detection facilities being made available through private and community funding to women of all socioeconomic levels, and with an increased awareness of the need for regular self-examination, larger numbers of women are being treated in the minimal stage and will fall into the 95 percent category with less disfigurement. Much of the credit for this increasingly hopeful outlook is to be given to women of the caliber of Mrs. Ford and Mrs. Rockefeller, whose courage, concern, and forthrightness have set an example for women in all walks of life.

Foreword

For awhile, the mass media promoted a technique called lump-ectomy, hailing it as a viable alternative to the mastectomy. Although most surgeons who temporarily advocated the lump-ectomy have since rejected it as adequate treatment when *any* malignancy was present, the press has not been as responsible in reporting the tragic failure of the lumpectomy. This is especially disheartening in view of the courage displayed by the mass media in bringing the importance of early detection to the attention of the public.

In spite of the proven progress we have seen within the past decade and the continued success we realistically anticipate for the future, the word *mastectomy* still carries connotations more appropriate to the Dark Ages and Gothic novels than it does to the living, breathing reality of the nearly one million (at an educated guess) women who are today leading active, fulfilled lives as a result of successful treatment of breast cancer by mastectomy.

To all of us who perform breast surgery, even more rewarding than the *quantity* of lives we have saved and are continuing to save is the *quality* of those lives, as evidenced by the statements of countless women to the effect that the mastectomy itself became the catalyst of a fuller appreciation and enjoyment of life itself.

This is the first book I have seen that offers concrete help with the problems of day-to-day adjustment faced by a post-mastectomy woman and takes into consideration different life-styles and socioeconomic statuses, relating the experience to the individual woman. It also rips away the veil of the hushed whisper attitude, which is the basis of the needless dread and anxiety experienced by the woman prior to and following a mastectomy.

I would recommend this book not only to women who have undergone mastectomies or are contemplating the possibility of one, but to everyone who is eager to help a post-mastectomy woman live her life to the fullest, whether that person be husband, mother, sister, son, co-worker, neighbor, friend, or patient.

That means all of us.

JEROME A. URBAN, M.D.
Acting Chief, Breast Service
Memorial Hospital for Cancer and Allied Diseases
New York City

Acknowledgments

I gratefully acknowledge the assistance and cooperation of members of the staff of Memorial Hospital for Cancer and Allied Diseases in New York City in reviewing the medically related material in this book. The American Cancer Society was of invaluable help in making their records and files available to me. The assistance of my sister-in-law, Pauline Winkler, also was invaluable in my technical research. The encouragement, patience, and inspiration of my many friends played a major role in bringing this book into being. To the surgeon whose astuteness and foresight saved my life, I can only say, "Of the Most High cometh healing."

Introduction

In 1973 I was ordered into the hospital for biopsies on both breasts. Twenty years before I had seen my mother die, a year after having had a radical mastectomy. That year was filled with despair, depression, and a general state of hopelessness. As a youngster, I had been unable to cope with my mother's problems, and this added to my own problem of having to stand by hopelessly and accomplish nothing.

Twenty years, I knew, had brought about radical advances in the detection and treatment of breast cancer and, I had hoped, help for the woman in the midst of problems surrounding a mastectomy. I was determined to take a constructive approach in dealing with my own possible double mastectomy, both in preparation and in life adjustment afterwards.

While hot lines are available to those with problems of drugs, alcoholism, and venereal disease, counseling services for the woman who fears the loss of one or both breasts are, at this writing, nonexistent for the most part.

Thanks to the astuteness of my surgeon in always insisting that I see him for regular checkups, he was able to catch the malignancy in its earliest stages. Subsequently I had a modified radical mastectomy on my right breast; my left side was spared. While my physical recovery was rapid, I was left with the anxiety of facing a totally new adjustment to life. As a single, self-supporting woman living in New York City, my questions were endless. Would I continue to be self-supporting? Would I be able to run my home alone? What about my relationships with men? In other words, would the life my surgeon had saved hold any meaning for me?

Where could I go for help in coping with these problems? Well-meaning efforts to cheer me up on the part of my friends only heightened my feelings of isolation. The Reach to Recovery Division of the American Cancer Society claimed that its services met the needs of the post-mastectomy woman. The program unquestionably has helped the large number of women whose major concern is "Will my husband continue to love me?" Their philosophy is painfully inadequate for the woman whose priorities are more on the order of "Will a man remain with me out of pity?" The confident whisper of "No one ever need know you had a mastectomy" is totally unrealistic when applied to the problems of a working woman. My efforts to enlist the interest of mass media in spotlighting the needs of the younger, physically active, unmarried, self-supporting woman were largely ignored. As in the case of the surrounding problems of the surgery itself, I discovered that the reality was simply not as bad as the dread. That's why I decided to write this book.

Working on this book, I have encountered people in all walks of life: industrial and civic leaders, post-mastectomy women as well as non-mastectomy women. And they each had one basic question: "What can *I* do to help the post-mastectomy woman?"

As a result of their efforts, services are now available to the post-mastectomy woman that were undreamed of in 1973. Boutiques serving the needs of post-mastectomy women have sprung up. Dance, exercise, and swimming programs have been developed for the post-mastectomy woman. Lingerie manufacturers have designed special brassieres and pads and are making them available for distribution in major department stores and specialty shops throughout the country, when, formerly, only about 40 percent of all women undergoing mastectomies received such products from hospitals or volunteer organizations. Even beauty salons are providing special medically approved services.

Besides manufacturers and civic leaders, I have spoken to scores of post-mastectomy women themselves, ranging from the twenty-three-year-old mother of a toddler to a eighty-three-year-old grandmother. I have spoken to housewives, celebrities, women on limited budgets as well as financially secure women, women who wanted their mastectomies kept secret, and women who felt they had every reason to be proud. It was these women who helped me avoid the trap of assuming that every experience was exactly like mine and who made sure that my book provided options for women of varying life-styles and ideas. These people enabled me to broaden my own perspective, which will, I hope, in the long run, spur healthy, open attitudes on the part of my readers and the general public.

Phase I
YOU'VE
WON HALF
THE BATTLE

1
The Mastectomy Mystique

Practically speaking, no woman ever goes into the hospital for a mastectomy. She goes in for a biopsy, with crossed fingers and a sense of terror, hoping against hope that it will turn out to be nothing. She goes with the virtuous reassurance of well-meaning friends that she has "nothing to worry about." True, in a fraction of a percent of all cases, a woman does go into the hospital knowing that she will have a mastectomy, but this is a result of having undergone a biopsy a few days before, and further scrutiny of the slide under a microscope having revealed that former reports of nonmalignancy were inaccurate.

In either case, no woman is prepared to take constructive action in advance to help herself cope realistically with the mastectomy and all its implications. Fortunately, four out of five women who enter the hospital for a biopsy emerge with both breasts and, although the experience may have been harrowing for them, at least they have had the official word on the "all clear." Even the experience of the biopsy itself, whether or not a mastectomy is involved, can have a devastating effect on a woman. The process of suspicion, X rays, and sweating out the report can easily add up to emotional crucifixion by the time she reaches the hospital.

Questions like "Am I going to die?" "If I live, will I lose my womanhood?" "Will I be an invalid for the rest of my life?" if voiced, will only provoke reactions of shocked horror and disapproval. "You mustn't even think of such a thing" and "You've got to take a positive approach" are stock answers. Unspoken fear, however, can be even more disastrous, as anxieties turn inward to fester.

Even the woman whose anxious queries are met with the response that the possibility of a mastectomy *could* exist, is usually given the answers, "My mother's cousin had a mastectomy twenty years ago and she's fine today," or "My friend's neighbor had a mastectomy two years ago and you ought to see her on the tennis court now." Other people will point with pride to the wonderful adjustment made by the politically prominent women whose recovery from mastectomy was bolstered by the support and good wishes of the entire nation. Intellectually, we are aware that other women have undergone mastectomies and are leading meaningful lives.

But none of us could put in a hasty phone call to a politician's wife or a friend's mother's cousin to ask about a mastectomy. Like the Victorian attitude toward pregnancy and childbirth, such details are things that nice people simply don't talk about. While today no pregnant woman would hesitate to discuss such topics as where to buy maternity clothes, discomforts accompanying pregnancy, and delivery itself, the woman contemplating a mastectomy has no one with whom she can share confidences. Unless the woman has a sister or close friend who has undergone a mastectomy, she feels totally isolated. Even if she were in contact with another woman who had undergone a mastectomy, a woman under thirty would find it difficult to confide in the woman who had her mastectomy after her children were grown.

Our culture does not permit open discussion of fears and anxieties where the possibility of serious illness or even of death exists. While it is acceptable to discuss fears such as the loss of a job, the breakup of a marriage or some other close relationship, or even a feeling of personal inadequacy, the woman who fears the loss of a breast is met only by the anxieties of others who cannot face the problem themselves. Today, fortunately, a woman with a breast problem is urged to seek medical advice promptly. Yet few women feel they can approach their surgeons with such questions as "How will I be able to run my home?" "Will my husband consider me repulsive?" and "Why did this have to happen to me?"

Nor does the woman contemplating a mastectomy have any assistance from the mass media. There is no telephone number she can call any hour of the day or night to have her questions answered. Thoughts of suicide, which are often experienced by people when confronted with the word *cancer*, are turned inward. On top of our own fears are added the anxieties we feel in relation to those close to us. "Suppose they knew how I *really* feel?" Is it any wonder that we feel compelled to put on a performance that could earn us an Academy Award, at the expense of our sanity?

While contemplating a mastectomy, the woman who seeks objective, clear-thinking help from community resources finds herself pounding on doors that seemingly are locked to her. Reach to Recovery has no facilities for the pre-biopsy or pre-mastectomy woman. This organization was founded through the efforts of Mrs. Terese Lasser, who underwent a mastectomy in 1952 and discovered that services for post-mastectomy women were virtually nonexistent. She created a one-woman campaign to bring some form of nonmedical help to the mastectomy patient. As a result of Mrs. Lasser's efforts, countless women have received special brassieres and soft breast forms to be worn immediately following surgery which would otherwise have been unavailable to them. Also, these women were visited in the hospital by fully recovered mastectomy women. But it is in the area of recovery exercises that Terese Lasser may go down in history as "the mother of post-mastectomy recovery," much as Joseph Lister has been named "the Father of Surgery."

However, the Reach to Recovery program evokes mixed reactions among those in the medical profession, and many doctors, while conceding the merits of the exercises, are reluctant to have their patients approached by a Reach to Recovery volunteer, while others automatically authorize volunteers to visit their patients. Either attitude is a mixed blessing. There are undoubtedly countless women who could have benefited from Reach to Recovery services but whose doctors did not approve, just as a number of women who were visited automatically by Reach to Recovery volunteers, without their prior knowledge or approval, found the experience trying, to say the least.

Reach to Recovery's philosophy that only a post-mastectomy woman can understand the problems of another mastectomy woman is not shared by everyone. As most of the volunteers represent a particular life-style, which might best be described as upper middle class, too many women from other socioeconomic and cultural levels have felt that their priorities were completely bypassed. After all, no one would suggest that an upper-middle-class suburban mother visit the wife of an unemployed laborer who had just given birth to her eighth unplanned child to give her a pep talk about the joys of motherhood.

Reach to Recovery is in no way to be blamed for this. Statistically, for many years, the highest number of mastectomies was performed on upper-middle-class women. This was due, in part, to the fact that women in this bracket tended to consult with doctors more frequently, even before symptoms became too pronounced. Thanks to the courage of a few nationally prominent women and the concern of people like Dr. Philip Strax and other founders of the Guttman Institute in New York City and in the other detection centers it has spawned throughout the country, the gift of life is being extended to women on all income levels.

But as to the needs of either the pre-mastectomy or post-mastectomy woman, the cruelest slap in the face emanates from the quarter that prides itself on its concerns for the needs of women—what is loosely known as the women's movement. As of this writing, the women's movement seems to dismiss the question of mastectomies as "unnecessary," offering the surgical placebo of lumpectomy, a medical treatment in vogue for awhile but since rejected by its original proponents. Unfortunately, the lumpectomy process has not been buried as quickly as some of its victims have been.

It is to be hoped that hospital and civic groups will become aware of the needs of the pre-biopsy patient as they did those of the pregnant woman, who today is offered all the preparation she needs for the process of childbirth as well as for postnatal care.

In the meantime, several manufacturers have made efforts to aid the mastectomy patient in her immediate clothing needs. Today the woman who wakes up in the recovery room rather than the hospital room, indicating that a mastectomy was performed, can ask a close friend or relative to get her what she needs for her most basic comforts.

There is, however, at this writing, no government, civic, or private organization that offers a woman adequate preparation and practical knowledge prior to the possible need for a mastectomy. Reach to Recovery will not give any information or literature to a woman who is scheduled for a biopsy. Their stock answer is, "If you should need a mastectomy, we'll have a volunteer visit you in the hospital to answer all your questions." Hospitals will only answer questions about admission policy, i.e., what insurance identification to bring. Surgeons will only answer medically related questions, and it is highly unlikely that a woman would feel comfortable asking her surgeon about practical needs such as clothing and how to run her home.

It is because of generally glib evasiveness to the needs of a woman before she enters the hospital that the entire mastectomy process is still surrounded by so much unnecessary emotional upheaval, most of which could be circumvented by adequate and realistic preparation.

2
First Steps in the Hospital

You've won half the battle.

No matter how much discomfort, annoyance, and pain you may be going through, there's a certain inner satisfaction in knowing that you've made it. You've pulled through. This was probably your greatest unexpressed fear when you learned that you were going into the hospital for a possible mastectomy. There is a certain sense of relief in knowing that something you've dreaded is actually behind you. But, as in every instance of major surgery, you're suddenly overcome with a feeling of helplessness, and immediate problems overshadow everything else.

"What did they do to me?" is one of the first questions you will ask yourself. "What is the mystery that lurks beneath the bandages?" You have heard so many conflicting whispers surrounding the word *mastectomy.* Following is a list of categories of mastectomies, but remember, there are gradations in between, and although two women could fall into the category of standard radical, it is probable that their operations would not be identical.

Partial Mastectomy:

The partial mastectomy is also called a biopsy, a local excision, a lesion excision, or a lumpectomy.* This is what we all refer to as

---

*Although the word *lumpectomy* is sometimes used to describe this procedure, it is not accepted as a viable mode of treatment if any malignancy has been found.

the biopsy, and if no malignancy has been discovered, no further treatment is required. Scarring is minimal, breast size is rarely affected, and there will be no arm disability. (However, you might want to have a lounge bra [page 111] and a wide-sleeved shirt [page 113] for your comfort following the brief hospital stay.)

Simple Mastectomy:

Removal of the breast only—lymph nodes, muscles, and chest wall are not affected. Arm exercises are not imperative.

Simple Mastectomy with Axillary Lymph Node Dissection:

Removal of the breast plus axillary lymph nodes. Arm exercises are indicated.

Modified Radical Mastectomy:

Removal of breast, lymph nodes, and secondary chest muscle (*pectoralis minor*). Arm exercises are necessary. (Thanks to improved detection measures, more mastectomies are falling into this category.)

Radical Mastectomy:

Also referred to as the standard radical. Although it is sometimes called the Halsted Radical, actually, the Halsted is merely one variation of the standard radical. This operation generally signifies removal of the breast, primary and secondary chest muscles (*pectoralis major* and *minor*), lymph nodes, and axillary pads. Some contour change can be expected due to muscle removal. Exercises for arm movement should begin as soon as your doctor approves.

Extended Radical Mastectomy:

In addition to the standard radical, excision of the chest wall or part of the rib cage may also be involved. This operation causes more contour change than the standard radical. Although most women are initially distressed upon learning that an extended radical has been performed, the dramatic increase in survival rates (see foreword) more than compensates for this first reaction. Arm exercises are indicated *as advised by your doctor.*

In addition to the foregoing, some mastectomies are performed with simultaneous silicone implants or with provisions for plastic surgery to be performed in the future. Your doctor probably discussed this with you before the biopsy. Arm exercises are required with an implant, according to your doctor's instructions.

"Will I ever be able to move again?" "How long will I have to wear these straitjacket bandages?" "Why did this have to happen to me, anyway?" "Why does this have to happen to *anyone*?" These questions seem to occur simultaneously.

You probably will want to greet your visitors with an air of "Don't worry, I'm doing OK." You would like to look fairly presentable but wonder if anyone at all in a hospital can look presentable. As you may not have been prepared for a hospital stay of more than a couple of days, you suddenly wonder if you have everything you need for your comfort and well-being. The following checklist could be a help to you in asking a friend to get you the things you will need for your hospital stay as well as for your first weeks at home.

- Loose, comfortable nightgown, preferably of opaque fabric
- Temporary bra and fibrefill breast form
- Flat-heeled, scuff-type slippers
- Cosmetics and personal care items
- Dry shampoo
- Disposable underpants
- Notepaper, envelopes, stamps, pen, personal address book
- Books or magazines
- Knitting, needlepoint, or embroidery
- Loose, wide-sleeved robe or kimono
- Deep-armhole, button-front shirt or blouse
- 3 bed-size pillows for sleeping
- 1 small pillow for daytime use. (This can be either a baby pillow or a small, decorative throw pillow. Make sure the covering is of a nonirritating fabric.)
- Food supply (if you plan to return to your own home)
- Medication (if your doctor has prescribed any)

When the nurse brings the tray around, eating suddenly becomes an abstract concept. You can't quite make the connection that the food on the tray is supposed to find its way inside you. Even if you only nibble at your first meal, try to show some interest when the dietitian brings the menu for future meals. Your doctor will probably recommend emphasis on protein, so keep meat, eggs, fish, cheese, and milk in mind when ordering.

Getting off the bed may seem the equivalent of climbing Mount Everest, but the sooner you get your body moving, the better are your chances of physical recovery. Ask a nurse to help you the first few times, even if it is only for a trip across the hall to the bathroom. Keeping your slippers on the small table near your bed will make it easier to get into them. Getting off the bed may seem relatively easy; it's getting back on that can appear to be an insurmountable problem—especially if the bed is high. A nurse may be able to help you with the problem of returning to bed. As most hospital beds have sides that can be raised, ask the nurse to put up the side of the bed away from the side you get out on. Standing with your back against the open side of the bed, place your hips against the mattress as though you were going to sit on it. With your nonoperative arm (the one unaffected by surgery), grab onto the raised side. Ease yourself into a firm sitting position on the mattress, and still holding the raised side, swing both legs up onto the bed. You can then ease yourself into a comfortable position.

At first, you will probably be visited only by those closest to you, but in a day or so you may find yourself besieged with a steady stream of visitors. If too many visitors are tiring to you, tell those closest to you to ask the others to wait until you get home. If you suddenly find yourself getting tired when your visitors are there, tell them you would like to rest for awhile and suggest that they go to the hospital cafeteria or a nearby coffee shop for a snack. Of course, you want to appear appreciative of their interest and concern, but at this time your first priority is *you*. This is no time for etiquette at the expense of your comfort. Your visitors will probably appreciate your telling them how you feel, but whether or not this is true, remember that they are actually waiting to take their cue from you.

Your immediate task in the hospital will be to get your arm back in motion. This may seem unthinkable, but it is your most crucial step toward recovery. Memorial Hospital in New York City is a leading research and treatment hospital for cancer in the country, and its Post-Mastectomy Rehabilitation Service serves as a model for hospitals throughout the nation. Patients at Memorial begin their exercise classes a day or two after surgery. These exercises were developed in conjunction with Reach to Recovery. Terese Lasser deserves credit not only for having developed her own arm exercises, which were subsequently modified to meet the needs of all mastectomy patients, but for convincing so many hospitals of the need for this form of therapy. Although the medical profession has long recognized the necessity for starting these exercises as soon after surgery as possible to prevent the possibility of a "frozen shoulder" and as an aid in drainage of the wound, Dr. J. Herbert Dietz, Jr., director of the Post-Mastectomy Rehabilitation program at Memorial, feels that the exercises serve an additional purpose as well. According to Dr. Dietz, "The sooner the patient regains her physical capacity and independence, the less tendency she has to regard herself as an invalid, with the surrounding depression that inevitably follows." If your hospital does not have a formal post-mastectomy program, a nurse or other hospital staff member may show you how to do the arm exercises. Possibly a Reach to Recovery volunteer may visit you and instruct you in the exercises and leave you a booklet. *Always check with your doctor as to which exercises are suitable for you.* In your particular case, it may not be advisable for you to attempt to raise your arm higher than shoulder level in the beginning. Also, you may want to try some of the exercises described in chapter 13 as an adjunct to the ones the hospital prescribes for you. Here again, *do not attempt these or any other exercises for the arm or total body until your doctor gives his or her approval.*

The answers to the following questions that you might want to ask your doctor will be helpful in obtaining for you a perspective on your immediate goals and needs.

• Is any specific diet recommended for your return home?
• Are there any prescriptions to be filled?
• Is there any special precaution relating to arm care, such as promoting drainage or preventing swelling?
• Are there any arm exercises you should be doing?
• Are there any exercises you should *discontinue*?
• Which of the exercises in chapter 13 are advisable?
• Are there any restrictions on traveling or short trips?

Your hospital may provide you with a temporary brassiere and fibrefill breast pad to wear until you are ready to have a more permanent prosthesis and brassiere. In some cities, a Reach to Recovery volunteer will provide you with the temporary bra and form.

If this temporary bra and form are not provided, a friend or relative will be able to buy them for you at a local corset shop or department store. Confidante and Jodee are two leading manufacturers of post-mastectomy brassieres and prostheses, and they are both making an all-out effort to meet the immediate needs of the post-mastectomy woman. These temporary bras and forms are illustrated and described in full detail in chapter 14, "Clothes." If a local shop does not carry them, a list of the suppliers in your area can be obtained from the manufacturers. Shopping information can be found in Appendix C.

You may want to wear this temporary brassiere and form in the hospital for comfort and appearance. With the bandages on, the form may seem too large to match your existing breast. Some of the fibrefill can be removed, but save it in the plastic bag in which it comes, as you will want to reshape it later, when the bandages come off. Although this fibrefill form was designed for temporary use, many women always keep at least one handy for sleeping, use in bathing suits, and as a general "reserve" form. There are also quite a few women who prefer this form to a more formal and expensive prosthesis.

You will undoubtedly be thinking of what kind of prosthesis and brassiere to wear after you are healed. If a Reach to Recovery volunteer visits you, she will probably give you information and literature on the types available and go on to recommend a specific type for you. Being fitted for a prosthesis and brassiere is not your immediate problem, and when the time comes this is one of the questions you will discuss with your surgeon. Although many doctors leave the decision up to the woman's preference and comfort, there are certain prostheses—often the heavily weighted and more expensive ones—that are contraindicated in certain cases. Also, your doctor may recommend one type of brassiere over another. For certain types of surgery and, depending upon the physical makeup of the woman, a built-up shoulder, wide-strap bra may be indicated. These are described in chapter 15, "The Prosthesis." Remember, this decision is to be based on your surgeon's advice, *not* the advice of another post-mastectomy woman or the fitter in the corset shop.

Another immediate concern is comfortable, presentable clothing while you are in the hospital. Because of the difficulty of arm motion, getting a robe on over a nightgown presents a problem. Regenesis and Empire State Mastectomy Salon are two mastectomy boutiques located in New York. They offer nightgowns for comfortable in-hospital as well as post-hospital wear. Their services are described in chapter 14, and some of their nightgowns are illustrated there as well.

Personal comfort is a major consideration while you are in the hospital. Bandaged as you are, a shower or tub bath is out of the question, and washing your hair presents a particular problem. Some hospitals provide hairdressing services with specially trained operators visiting the patient at bedside. Even if you are not accustomed to having your hair set, a shampoo may make you feel more comfortable. If this doesn't appeal to you, perhaps a dry shampoo is the answer. Pssst and Minipoo are two such products available. These are powdered substances that are brushed through the hair.

Disposable underpants are a convenience during a hospital stay. Although they are designed to be used during menstruation, many women have found them invaluable for traveling or in other situations where laundry could become a problem. Morning Gloree is a popular brand and is available in packages of four for about $1 in drug and department stores.

Flat nonskid slippers are advisable following any form of major surgery. Terrycloth scuffs are inexpensive and easy to slip in and out of. They are available in notion stores, some drug and sundries stores, and department stores. Some lingerie stores also carry them.

Throughout your hospital stay, your doctor (as well as the entire medical team) will encourage you to use your affected arm as much as possible, especially in activities that involve raising it, such as brushing your hair. If your "working" arm was affected (i.e., right arm if you are right-handed), you are in a position to provide yourself with therapy in the form of ordinary activity. Writing thank-you notes for get-well cards and flowers is also excellent exercise for your arm. In addition to its therapeutic advantages, you will be glad you got these little details out of the way when you get home! Your hospital may provide occupational therapy. Sewing, weaving, knitting, crochet, and needlepoint will help get your arm back in motion. If it is your nonworking arm that is affected, try using it for brushing your hair and other personal care activity. Your doctor will probably recommend keeping your arm raised, preferably on a pillow, as much as possible, in order to promote drainage. You will probably sleep with your affected arm on a pillow or two as well.

After a few days on your feet, you'll be thinking about immediate post-hospital plans. As a mastectomy is not always a foreseeable hospital stay, such as having a baby or previously decided-upon surgery such as an appendectomy, not everyone makes arrangements for immediate post-hospital needs. If you live alone, or even if you have a family with children of a self-sufficient age, there may be at least one relative or friend who will urge you to stay with her immediately upon leaving the hospital. If you have young children, someone may offer to stay with you during the first few weeks. These possibilities should be given very careful consideration. After the sterile atmosphere of a hospital, you may want to get back to your favorite and familiar things. You might not feel too comfortable in anyone's home but your own. If your mother or mother-in-law offers to stay with you, it could mean an added emotional strain, although a reduced physical one.

If you feel that staying with a friend or relative could be beneficial, there are traps that should be avoided. The tendency of well-meaning friends not to let you lift a finger is not going to do much for your physical recovery or self-respect. If you do decide to stay with someone, discuss beforehand what your role will be. Make it clear that you cannot be waited on hand and foot, and tell your hostess which tasks you would like to do yourself. Many ordinary household tasks will be beneficial to your arm and total body movement. If your hostess has a dishwasher, explain to her that you would like to wash and dry a few dishes. Although you will not be lifting or moving a vacuum cleaner, ask to do some of the vacuuming once the vacuum cleaner has been set up. You might ask to take charge of preparing some meals, requesting that someone be with you to lift heavy items or obtain dishes from high shelves.

If you're returning home to a husband and family, especially if you have young children, a close relative may insist on staying with you. Consider this very carefully. The feeling of being mistress of your own home is important during this period. If your children are of junior high or high school age, they can help with the running of your home, and if they've never done it before, this is an excellent opportunity for them to start. As in the case of staying with a relative, if your husband and children conspire to prevent you from lifting a finger, explain to them that it is important for your recovery that you do as many tasks as you are able to do.

If you're living with your husband or another adult, explain that you will be asking his or her help for certain activities but that it is important that you do as much for yourself as possible.

Although you will probably eventually be able to wear most of your clothes, the combination of heavy bandages and limited arm use will necessitate easier, looser, more comfortable clothes. A front-closing, deep-armhole shirt is essential for the period immediately following surgery. You already may have such a shirt in your wardrobe. If not, the subject is fully covered in chapter 14. It would be a good idea to have a friend bring you such a shirt while you are still in the hospital.

If you work or are active in civic affairs, you might want to appoint a close friend or relative to advise people that you have had surgery and will keep them informed as to when you will again become active. Although post-mastectomy women are frequently advised, "You don't have to tell anyone if you don't want to"—the hushed whisper approach—I cannot recommend trying to keep a mastectomy a secret. Only a woman who leads a cloistered existence, pampered by household help and family members, could successfully take such a closet approach to her mastectomy. To live with the dread question, "Will anyone know?" can only create added emotional problems. A constant fear of being found out can create more problems than the mastectomy itself.

When you leave the hospital, anticipation of resuming everyday responsibilities can appear to be overwhelming, but remember, in every phase of recovery it's best to go one step at a time.

3
First Steps at Home

When you arrive home, the lists of do's and don'ts, the details of running a home, dealing with visitors, making arrangements for postoperative visits to the doctor's office, wondering how you're going to cope with only limited use of one arm, may all seem staggering. But, as you got through first steps in the hospital by coping with one thing at a time, you will also see yourself through this transitional period. In addition, asking your doctor the following questions will give you a clearer idea of your own limitations and capabilities.

- Which arm exercises should be continued?
- Which arm exercises should be discontinued?
- What steps can be taken to prevent swelling of the affected arm?
- When will you be able to drive?
- When will you be able to return to work?
- Any restrictions on traveling—by car, train, or airplane?
- When can you take part in a medically approved post-mastectomy exercise program?
- What should you do if you sustain a burn or infection on the arm or operative side?

For the record, I list below the usual precautions that apply to every post-mastectomy patient. (Your doctor will advise you of any additional ones in your case.)

- *Avoid cuts, bruises, scratches, and burns in the affected arm.**
    Use a thimble for sewing.
    Wear protective gloves for gardening.
    Do not use cuticle scissors or in any way attempt to remove or tamper with the cuticle on the affected hand.
    Wear rubber gloves for household tasks, especially those involving detergents or steel wool.
    Avoid injections and vaccinations on the affected arm.
    Take care of minor cuts and scratches immediately. Wash area and cover with protective dressing.
    Use padded mitts when handling hot utensils or reaching into the oven.
- *Avoid constriction in the affected arm.*
    Do not have blood pressure taken on the affected arm.
    Keep jewelry loose—bangle bracelets rather than exotic armbands—and avoid tight wristwatch straps.
    Avoid tightness in sleeves and underarm seams.
- *Avoid carrying heavy packages with the affected arm.*
- *Avoid narrow, tight brassiere straps that create a tourniquet effect.*
- *Avoid overexposure to direct sunlight.*
    Tan gradually—avoid sunburn.
    Keep sweater or other covering handy for the affected arm.
- *Avoid beauty care products containing hormones.*
- *Consult with your surgeon before taking any hormone-related medication or contraceptive pills.*
- *Examine remaining breast and skin over chest area once a month. Report any changes to your surgeon.*

HYGIENE AND BEAUTY CARE

Personal care and basic comfort at home require adjustments you never may have made before, especially if you never have had an accident, undergone surgery, or given birth. Restrictions on taking a bath or shower can be especially infuriating—even more

---

*The major function of the lymphatic glands is to fight infection. With the lymph nodes removed during mastectomy, the tendency toward infection (and, consequently, swelling) is increased. You will want to avoid all possible infection. Cuticle scissors—or even pushing the cuticle with a stick—can create problems.

so for the woman who has regarded soaking in a tub as part of her private luxury routine. However, the bandages being what they are, we simply have to make do.

If you don't have anyone to help you in and out of the tub, at least make sure you have good grip supports. Also, a nonskid mat in the tub, as well as a nonskid bath mat for stepping out of the tub, will help to avoid accidents. The tub should be filled only to below-waist level when seated. A bath sponge, synthetic or natural, carefully wrung out, will avoid dripping on the bandaged area.

Shampooing presents a particular problem, especially for the woman who is accustomed to washing her hair several times a week. Handheld shower attachments can be purchased for as little as $1 in discount stores, or up to about $35 for sophisticated chrome arrangements in department stores and specialty closet shops. If you have someone to help you, this attachment can be used while you are leaning forward over the tub. If you feel that shampooing at home can be a problem, you can make an arrangement with a local hairdresser for wash and dry services only, without setting. This is usually quite inexpensive, especially if you don't make an appointment for a Friday or Saturday, and goes a long way in giving you a general feeling of freshness.

In New Jersey, a rapidly expanding chain of beauty salons called Stage Hairdressers is making a special service available to post-mastectomy women. This includes the wash and dry only, if desired, as well as a setting that uses pump-type dispensers for hair-setting lotion rather than aerosol spray cans, whose fine mists, inevitably inhaled, create lung irritation. None of the beauty products used for facials contain any hormones. The cuticle is not touched in any way on the affected arm during manicures. A particular detail of concern on the part of the owners is the availability of small, towel-covered pillows for the woman who needs to keep her arm raised.

The owners of Stage Hairdressers have recently opened a training school for beauticians, where every student will be trained in the post-mastectomy service so that it will eventually spread to all parts of the country. Currently their services are available in Closter, Dumont, Paramus, and Oakland, New Jersey. For the woman whose visits to the hairdresser are a regular part of her routine, making a sudden change in beauty salons could be upsetting at this time. For this reason, the owners of Stage Hair-dressers are making details of their service available to beauticians throughout the country. If your beauty salon would like to provide this service, the owner can contact Mr. Adam Slepp, Beauty School of Bergen County, Promenade Level, Bergen Mall, Paramus, New Jersey 07652.

CLOTHING

You've undoubtedly been told that eventually you'll be able to wear all your clothes, or at least most of them. For such things as bathing suits and evening gowns, you may be apprehensive about the extent of the scar or possible disfigurement. Ask your doctor about this. While chapter 14 is devoted to clothes, both for immediate postop and when you are fully healed; comfort and ease of action is the prime requisite for the interim period. Although you have a loose-fitting robe or housecoat, wearing regular daytime clothing may do more for your morale. The deep-armhole shirt will become almost your uniform during this period. As you regain arm motion, you will ease your way back into wearing regular clothes; dresses with loose, wide sleeves are ideal. Dresses that have back zippers could be a problem; but there is a gadget sold in sewing and notion stores that could be of help. It's called the Dritz Zipper Pull and sells for about $.50. It does facilitate one-handed zipping.

Even if you have someone to help you with dressing, you will want to become as self-sufficient as possible. Although button-front clothing is the easiest during this time, there can still be a problem with movement of the arm. The routine I worked out for dressing myself in the deep-armhole shirt is as follows: Keep the operative arm slightly bent and work the sleeve on that side up to the shoulder. Standing with your back near a wall, pull the shirt across your back and lean against the wall. You will easily be able to slide into the other sleeve.

Although people will rush to help you on with a coat or jacket, they are largely unaware that the operative arm cannot always be moved back easily to fit into a coat that is held at the shoulders. Explain to your friend that you will start the process yourself, then ask for help. Here again, work the sleeve for the operative arm on up to the shoulder and ask your friend to hold the coat for you while you get your other arm into the sleeve.

The temporary bra and fibrefill pad will be your mainstay during the period in which you are healing. As the bandages become less cumbersome, you will replace some of the filling into the pad, filling it out, as necessary, to match the remaining breast. Although both the bra and pad are washable and dry relatively quickly, you will probably want to own at least one more of each, especially if you find it more comfortable to sleep with them on. In chapter 14 two "interim" bras are described and illustrated—the Jodee Lounge Bra, Style No. 500, and the Confidante Gentle Fit, Style No. 493. The Confidante gives slightly firmer support. If you own the Jodee, you may want to have the Confidante as your second bra, and vice versa.

RESTING

Your doctor probably advised you to keep your operative arm elevated as much as possible. While a bed-size pillow would be too cumbersome for daytime use, a small decorative throw pillow, covered in a nonirritating fabric, is attractive as well as functional and can be used when visiting as well as at home. Also, baby pillows, available in infant departments of department stores, are comfortable, and the pillowcases can be changed frequently. A couch is ideal for arm elevation. Merely rest your operative arm on the back of the couch or chair, with your upper arm resting on the pillow.

SLEEPING AND SEXUAL ACTIVITY

Sleeping may present problems for the post-mastectomy patient. Ideally, you should have two bed-size pillows for the operative arm, another one for under your head and, in many cases, a pillow under the other arm for aiding in comfort and balance. This can make a total of four bed-size pillows. The woman who has been accustomed to sleeping flat on her back should experience only a minimum of discomfort. However, the woman who considers comfortable sleeping to include a variety of positions—on her stomach, on her side, or frequent changes of positions during the night—is going to have to make an adjustment during this period.

It would be difficult to bring up the question of sleeping without discussing the problems of sharing a bed. Unless you share a king-size bed, your partner will not only begin to feel crowded out, but will become apprehensive that he or she may inadvertently bump into you while you're both asleep. During this period, if you could have a bed to yourself, it could ease anxiety all around. If you have a guest room or a sofa-bed in the living room, this could provide the answer. Whether you would be more comfortable in the big bed or in a smaller one can be discussed between you and your partner.

But, as we cannot discuss the subject of sleeping without mentioning the possibility (or, more likely, probability) of sharing a bed, neither can we discuss the question of sharing a bed without bringing up the subject of sex. Although this matter will be delved into more deeply in chapter 17, I feel I should say a few words here about the question of resuming sexual activity and dressing in front of your partner.

Of course, there are no medical restrictions on sexual activity, and your doctor will probably recommend resumption as soon as possible, if you should ask about it. According to some of the soap-opera attitudes regarding post-mastectomy women, sexual relations are to be resumed practically the moment a woman emerges from anesthesia, but stories are told about women who literally hide in the closet in order to get undressed.

Because of the trauma of the experience and its connotations as a threat to sexuality (unfounded, as we all eventually learn), I cannot go along with the idea that a woman is to be forced to put on an act that she doesn't feel has meaning, or that her husband or lover should be coerced into acting as though nothing has happened. Remember, the man in your life is going through his own set of anxieties and bewilderment; there probably exists the desire to do the right thing, combined with total confusion as to what the right thing is.

If you feel comfortable dressing and undressing in the presence of a man and can ask for his help, so much the better. But if you're going through a period where you cannot fully face the fact yourself, it can be a relief all around if you tell him you'd rather not undress in his presence at this time, rather than feel obliged to sneak furtively into the bathroom. Whether or not sexual relations are resumed immediately, you can explain to him that it would be more considerate of you both if you were to sleep in a bed of your own, not only until you're able to do without the pillows, but until the double bed can have the meaning it had prior to your surgery. Feeling free enough to openly discuss your need to abstain from sexual relations for a limited time probably can go a lot further in building the foundations for future shared intimacy than any forced desire to please, on your part or his.

Especially for the woman to whom sexual activity meant total body involvement, the idea of making love with the upper part of her body practically immobilized can be slightly repugnant, to say the least. However, in instances where one partner may have any physical problems at all, including a back problem, methods can be worked out between two understanding adults whereby the needs of both partners are fully met.

The same nightgown you had in the hospital can serve as well at home, as can, for that matter, any way of sleeping that you regard as comfortable, including wearing nothing at all. Whether or not you decide to sleep in the lounge bra and form, or a nightgown with a "puff" (see chapter 14) depends on your own comfort. But if you do decide to sleep in a nightgown, pajama top, or loose housecoat, you will probably feel more content in an opaque cotton or synthetic fabric. Putting on a frilly, frothy nightgown over the bandages is hardly to be recommended. Although it may seem remote to you now, there will again be a time when you will be wearing soft, feminine nightgowns.

DOMESTIC PROBLEMS

We have so far discussed personal comfort and needs, but first steps at home include steps in easing back into day-to-day responsibilities and relationships with others.

If you live alone, the prospect of returning home can be frightening. As there was virtually no preparation for your trip to the hospital, many of the household tasks you had planned to do simply did not get done, and visions of dust, unturned mattresses, closets you had meant to clean out, and draperies that should have been taken to the cleaners seem overwhelming. The fact that you will be spending so much time at home, especially if you have been going to work, is going to make every speck of dust appear to be eight inches in diameter, and ceilings will suddenly look as though they have to be scrubbed.

If an adult and/or teen-age children live at home with you, they will be able to help you with many of the household tasks, but make it clear to them that your doing as much as possible is part of your total recovery.

If you have a family with young children or are a woman living alone, you may want to look into the possibility of household help, even if you have never had any before. Your state employment services or telephone directory, under the listing of House Cleaning, are good sources for domestic help. Even if you have someone to help you once a week for the first few weeks, it will serve to eliminate the feeling that the dirt is piling up. If this would be a hardship for you financially, or you simply do not feel comfortable at the thought of hiring someone to help you with the housework, teen-age neighbors are often happy to help you with some tasks for a moderate fee.

If food shopping means a drive to a shopping center, someone could help out. If you don't have a washing machine at home, a young neighbor could go to the local laundromat for you. If you don't know any teen-agers among your neighbors' and friends' children, a phone call to the placement counselor at your local high school could help you locate one. Also, the dean's office at a nearby college will have a list of students who want part-time work.

If your children are of preschool age, a local nursery school might make an arrangement whereby your child could attend for a half day once or twice a week. This would be a good break-in experience for a preschool-age child as well as a chance for you to have some necessary time for yourself.

If you live alone, you will probably be surrounded by friends who will want to do as much for you as possible, and even regard it as their moral obligation to do so. This can be tempting but will be the beginning of many instances in which you will have to learn to be polite but firm in explaining that the best thing for you is to do as much as possible yourself. If you live within walking distance of food shops, this could be a therapeutic experience for you. Living in New York City, the week I was home from the hospital, I made it a point to go out twice a day to local food stores. Even if you only go out for a quart of milk, it serves the function of an outing and adds to your feeling of self-sufficiency. Remembering the precaution against carrying heavy packages in the affected arm, I made it a point to carry a light package, even asking the storekeeper on occasion for separate bags for small items.

If food shopping means a drive to a shopping center and a friend or neighbor offers to do your shopping for you, tell him or her you would like to take part in the process. Make your own selection in the supermarket, and if you do stock-up type shopping, ask the store to give you several small packages instead of many larger ones, offering to pay for the extra bags, if necessary. Use a wheeled shopping cart to take your packages from the car to your house.

During your first weeks at home, you will have visitors who practically will offer to take over your kitchen for you, especially when entertaining. As your sense of self-sufficiency is important, try to explain to them how they can help instead. Ask them to bring fruit, crackers and cheese, cake, or whatever you usually serve with coffee. Have paper plates and cups on hand. Make the coffee yourself, but ask someone to carry the pot to the table. If you're tired and don't want people to stay too long, tell them so, or excuse yourself to go into another room and lie down. *Your guests will appreciate your telling them what your needs are.* Forced politeness on your part and theirs will only create a strained atmosphere all around.

Cooking is another area that can be eased into slowly, and adjustments can be made in your usual routine to make things easier on yourself during this period. First of all, ask your doctor if he recommends any particular diet, such as high protein, upon your return home. Your doctor may also prescribe some long-range diet restrictions, such as cutting down on salt intake or avoiding highly spiced foods (see chapter 11, "Diet"). Low salt stipulation is for women who may have a problem with fluid retention, which causes swelling and discomfort in the remaining breast. Highly spiced foods, immediately following any form of surgery, are not recommended for anyone.

Whether you cook for yourself or for a family, there are conveniences that can help you through this period. Although I am against convenience foods on principle because of their high cost in comparison to ingredients used, often low nutritional value, and chemical additives, there are many basic frozen foods, such as vegetables unadorned with sauces, that are nutritionally adequate and easy to prepare. Your neighborhood may have small specialty food shops that feature take-out foods, and some restaurants even may deliver. Plain broiled meats and fish are not only easy to prepare, they are healthier than those with elaborate sauces and gravies. Fresh fruits and vegetables not only eliminate cooking, they could well start you and your family on eating habits that will benefit everyone. We have all been cautioned against putting the operative arm into a hot oven or risking minor burns. Therefore, if you have a counter-top electric broiler, by all means use it for meats and fish. If you are using the oven, try to plan on using a dish or pot that can be removed with one hand if there is no one at home to help you. In any event, a potholder should be used. Be sure the potholder is made of a noninflammable material. Dacron or other synthetic filling can burst into flame without warning. So choose your potholders for safety rather than clever designs.

Throughout this period you will be visiting your doctor frequently for postoperative checkups. He will be advising you of your progress. He can tell you at which point to stop certain arm exercises, which you will be replacing with everyday activity. You can ask the doctor what the extent of your scar will be, so that you can get a better idea of the clothes you will be able to wear. If you drive, your doctor will tell you when you are able to resume driving, but first time out it would be a good idea to have a licensed driver accompany you for a short trip. Try to avoid peak traffic hours.

With your doctor's approval, this would be a good time to give serious consideration to total body exercises, either in a community program or at home. Remember, the bandages won't be on forever. Since the surgery, you've been planning all your activity around the operative area. Beginning the total body exercises slowly will make you aware of "regaining" your body.

SOCIALIZING

You will probably find that you tire easily and it will be wisest for you to get all the rest you need. Because you don't feel that you

are your usual self, you may be reluctant to accept social invitations and are quite sensible to avoid overtiring yourself.
However, if you discuss your situation with your host or hostess
beforehand, you can arrange to attend social gatherings according
to your needs. During this time you want to get out and need a
change of scene but may be reluctant to face what you think will be
stares or ill-concealed expressions of pity. You might have the
feeling that you cannot totally participate in what is going on.
These occasions will be much easier if you've told people about the
surgery. Make it clear to your host that you may leave early, or
during the evening might go to another room to rest for short
periods. You will do better breaking in at a more informal
gathering, where casual dress will set the tone. The loose cotton
shirt, with perhaps a silk scarf tucked in at the neckline, and simple
slacks or a skirt will be both comfortable and attractive. Take your
small pillow with you and sit on chairs or couches where you can
rest your arm on the back. Also, offer to participate in as many
activities as you can and offer to pass around dishes or small trays
of snacks.

As you get out into the world, the question of "Whom do I tell?"
goes beyond merely those closest to you. The hushed whisper
approach to mastectomies, with the assurance of "Nobody has to
know," reminiscent of pregnancy during Victorian times, can only
place an added burden on an already emotionally fraught experience. At first, we all wonder "Does anything show?" "Do they
all know?" Today, it is only a woman who leads a completely
secluded life who could keep major surgery a secret. No woman
who goes into the hospital for a biopsy can, with any certainty,
assure an employer or business associate that she will be out only
for a few days. This also does not imply that we have to tell every
store clerk or bus driver that we've had a mastectomy. There is a
difference between "Whom do I tell?" and "With whom do I
discuss my mastectomy?" Morbid curiosity seekers do abound, who
glut themselves on details of illness, accidents, and ill-fated love
affairs. You will do yourself a favor if you learn to say, "Thank you
for your interest, but this is a matter I discuss only with my
surgeon."

THE WORKING WOMAN

To the working woman, the question, "When can I go back to work?" is uppermost in her mind. Whether it is the need for income, work piling up on your desk, the need to get back into the swing of things, or boredom with staying home, you will want to have some idea of when you can return to work and will want to advise your employer or associates of this. Like so many other questions, there is no set time and no set answer for everyone.

If at all possible, ease back into your working schedule slowly. Even if you go in for only an hour or two a day the first week, it can ease the transition for you. After staying home and a period of comparative inactivity for several weeks, the sudden transition to the nine-to-five routine can come as something of a jolt. If possible, try not to lose contact with your working associates during the time you are out. When you feel you can manage public transportation alone, arrange to meet some of your co-workers for lunch. This will give you a chance to break into public transportation gradually, starting with non-rush hours. It can be quite frightening to find yourself in the middle of a pushing crowd relatively soon after surgery. You may be concerned about bumping or jostling. With no outward identifying sign of the surgery, you will not receive the consideration people would be only too glad to give you if they knew. You have neither cane, crutch, nor sling to announce what you've recently been through.

Even when you are back at work full time, rush hours in public transportation will be frightening. Straphanging is not recommended for the operative arm. Even though you may have gained adequate motion in your arm, the sudden lurching of buses and subways could cause problems. Your area may have slower or local-stop transportation, which, although slightly more time-consuming, will add to your traveling comfort. If some degree of straphanging is inevitable, it may be advisable to switch to a small, lightweight handbag to carry just your basic essentials on your operative arm, so that the other one is free for holding onto straps and poles. As most of my own handbags tend to be of the suitcase variety, this was quite an adjustment for me.

THE SCAR

Seeing the scar for the first time is always a traumatic experience. The longer this is postponed, the larger the dragons of fear and dread seem to loom. On the other hand, glib advice such as, "Oh, come on, the scar isn't really all that bad," can be thoughtless and insensitive. It is not so much the scar itself that causes so much depression and anxiety as it is the fact that we are faced with the disappearance of the breast as well. For women who have previously had surgery, the sight of a scar is tempered with the knowledge that a fully healed scar is a far cry from a brand-new one. If the sight of the scar causes you to avoid mirrors and hide and makes you determined never to look in the mirror until you are fully dressed, you will be creating long-range problems for yourself. Try to bear in mind that the scar six months after surgery will be like any other scar you've ever seen on anyone. If surgeons or hospitals would provide patients with a series of photographs depicting scars from their new to their fully healed stages, much of this anxiety could be circumvented.

Most of us who had contemplated a mastectomy simply had visualized one day looking into a mirror and seeing one side of our chests flat. We just hadn't taken the interim process into consideration. If you feel, at this point, that the sight of the scar is something to which you will never be able to reconcile yourself, you might want to give some thought to the possibility of plastic surgery. This process is described in chapter 12, "All-Around Beauty Care." This is not a decision you have to make immediately, as most plastic surgery cannot be performed until about six months following the mastectomy. But even reading about it and knowing that you have that option if you feel you need it can go a long way toward convincing you that you may not have to spend the rest of your life "disfigured." However, like most post-mastectomy women, as the scar progressively fades you will find it difficult to look back and realize how upset you had been at first.

GETTING AWAY FROM IT ALL

When you've gotten back on your feet, your friends will be advising you about a vacation, and your need to get away, after all you've been through. Your hospitalization may have cut short some vacation plans you had made previously, either because of timing or, in many instances, for financial reasons.

Fortunately, the decision to take a vacation, and what kind, can be postponed until you are ready to consider all its aspects. Friends and relatives from out of town may urge you to spend a week or two with them as soon as you can travel comfortably. But it is best not to make definite commitments or plans until you are steadier on your feet. The invitations will hold indefinitely with your friends. People may encourage you to get away as soon as possible to "just go someplace and lie in the sun." If you go to a resort area where a lot of sport and physical activity is taking place and you are not able to participate, it will only increase your feeling of being left out. If you can afford it, or someone offers it to you, you may be thinking about international travel. This is something else that you may want to postpone until you feel you're able to enjoy it to the fullest. Try to wait until you've been in familiar surroundings for a while before you make any vacation plans. If the hospitalization has placed a severe strain on your finances, this does not mean that vacations are out indefinitely. Chapter 19, "Cultivating Enlightened Selfishness," offers suggestions for shorter, less expensive vacation plans.

Most important of all during this time is the realization that you are able to manage, and the understanding that the coming months will bring steady improvement and that you do have much to look forward to.

4
Anxiety and Depression

So far, we've discussed practical details merely for getting back on our feet again. Looking over the previous two chapters, anyone would think that a mastectomy could be likened to some sort of nuisance accident, such as breaking a leg while skiing, where the major problem might be, "How do I learn to maneuver steps with these crutches?" Most of us have learned by this time that the surgical aspects of the mastectomy carried a dread that was highly overrated, while the emotional aspects were unforeseen, never really voiced, and did not suddenly disappear when we realized that we had survived the surgery.

It could happen the day following surgery, two weeks after, or, in some cases, as long as two years following surgery. But whenever it happens, a reaction will set in. Trauma and shock are piled on top of one another. Conflicts within ourselves arise that we could not possibly have predicted. While the first reaction may well have been "Am I going to die?" this could well have been followed with "Do I want to live with only one breast?" Although our immediate concern the first time we went out of our homes may have been "Does anything show?" this could be followed by "Why can't people be more careful or show a little more concern?"

Whenever it happens, you know you've survived the surgery, and if you've been doing your exercises regularly, you have joined the ranks of mastectomy women whose general feeling seems to be that no such experience is ever to be taken lightly but that the dread was, by and large, uncalled for. But once you've gotten home from the hospital, everything seems to pile up, and you feel as though you can no longer escape or be distracted from all the thoughts and feelings you've been trying to avoid. The tension and anxiety that started from the day your doctor suggested a mammogram until you woke up to the reality that one or both breasts were gone would have taken enough of a toll. People have probably been telling you how lucky you are. You certainly don't feel that way at this point.

On top of the physical discomfort and emotional anxiety, there was the superefficient, depersonalized atmosphere of the hospital itself. Even if your physical recovery was rapid and smooth, you sometimes wonder if you'll ever recover from the hospital stay. It's easy to feel as though you were dissected into a hundred parts, with a hospital specialist assigned to one part only, so that while each part was scrutinized carefully, you felt that you were being completely bypassed as a human being.

Except possibly in the instance of an ill-advised love affair, we have probably never been put through an experience that created quite such a civil war within us between our sense of logic and our emotions. We tend to regard our emotions as the enemy—to be suppressed, denied, and above all hidden, like the proverbial skeleton in the closet. Although we would be forgiven a few discreet tears and sobs, we feel it is small consolation when we want to scream, kick, and rave.

In my own case, the rosy pictures people painted for me as to how well I was doing only increased my sense of outrage. Logic told me that I had taken the only sensible course of action open to me by seeking competent help when I did, and it was easier having the experience behind me than ahead. But the infuriating "Why did this have to happen to *me?*" seemed to blot out any rational thoughts I had been able to muster. On top of that, I had the feeling that something had been put over on me—that the decision was taken out of my hands. True, I signed for the mastectomy when I signed for the biopsy, but the feeling still remained that I was, somehow, "taken." Somehow, I would have liked to undo the whole process and wished I could wake up from the nightmare in the relief that the whole thing was a mistake.

Frequently, there was a free-floating resentment directed at whatever target came to my mind—the doctors, the hospital, the entire medical profession, as well as a few innocent bystanders. The operation was not preceded by any pain or discomfort, as frequently happens in the case of a tooth that has to be extracted. It was difficult to realize why the discovery of a tiny lump necessitated such drastic action. It seemed like the equivalent of having an arm removed because of a splinter in my finger.

Friends and relatives felt that their moral obligation was to cheer me up, or else I was greeted with an embarrassed, stammering "I really don't know what to say." Even worse, I felt that I was obligated to put on a brave front and answer false assurance with false reassurance. My guilt increased when I realized that those close to me were making an effort on my behalf and doing what they felt was right. It did not take too much memory to recall the numerous times when I had shifted nervously from foot to foot, not knowing what to say to someone who needed emotional support, whether it was because of a career disappointment or the loss of a close family member. However bumbling the attempts of friends might be (as my own once were), I felt that I owed them appreciation and gratitude.

The feeling on the part of a post-mastectomy woman that she is being treated as though she had an emotional lobotomy can also come into play. From a person whose opinion had been respected, we suddenly feel that we have been turned into a petulant child, who has to be calmed, placated, cajoled, and manipulated. In the name of "keeping her spirits up," we encounter veiled evasiveness and vague verbal placebos when we ask direct questions. The chuck-under-the-chin treatment that is given to us only increases our resentment and, consequently, our guilt, because we are aware that people are acting in what they believe to be our best interests.

Although the subject of mastectomies has come out of the closet as far as the need for detection and early treatment is concerned, as far as the mass media is concerned (or at least that segment of the mass media that acknowledges the fact that we had the right to undergo a mastectomy in the first place), the woman who actually has undergone a mastectomy is worthy of nothing more than a soap opera reaction. A sort of "mastectomy mystique" has been created by the more genteel segment of the women's press, based on emotional, tearful, happy-ending accounts of women emerging from the anesthesia to the assurance that yes, indeed, their husbands' love was steadfast, and, subsequently, these same husbands were totally indifferent to the loss of anything so insignificant as a breast, anyway. Misguidedly motivated to shower us with reassurance, people either gloss over glibly or deny altogether most of our real problems. For the lower- or middle-income woman, often self-supporting or responsible for the support of children, in addition to herself, as well as the unmarried woman, the life adjustment that must be made following a mastectomy is not the same as that of the suburban clubwoman who has never had to fill out an insurance company form.

The woman who was visited in the hospital by a Reach to Recovery volunteer was unquestionably appreciative of the brassiere and temporary form she was given, if they were given to her (not all chapters of Reach to Recovery provide this service). If her hospital did not have a physical therapy program, she was doubly grateful for the exercise instructions. But unless the woman's life-style duplicated that offered by the mastectomy soap opera, she was left with the feeling of having been patted on the head. Not every woman has the prerequisite "loving husband" (who invariably has a guaranteed income of $50,000 a year) who will continue to love her, thereby negating the effects of the mastectomy. Nothing is said about the husband (or lover) who may be confronted with his own problems triggered off by the mastectomy and, consequently, could use a little support himself. Even if the husband or lover were to cast himself into the role of fountain from which all emotional strength flowed, this could, in too many cases, serve as nothing more than a crutch. And, tragically, that crutch could prove to be made of papier maché.

Nevertheless, the anxiety-charged question, "Will I continue to be attractive to my husband?" is basic, especially to the younger woman and even more so to the unmarried woman who is trying to foresee future relationships. And for the married or unmarried woman alike, especially if she is pursuing an identity of her own rather than that of someone's wife or lover, the question "Will he leave me?" is eclipsed by a much more threatening one: "Will he stay with me out of pity?" In this instance, reassurances can only intensify feelings of dependence and inadequacy, or, worse still, the tendency toward paranoia that will manifest itself in thoughts like "He's covering up his revulsion out of politeness."

While in the hospital, virtually every fear that enters the patient's mind comes under the heading of unmentionable, where the hospital staff and, often, visitors are concerned. "Did they get it all?" "Was it too late?" and "How do I know there won't be a recurrence?" are usually met with supercilious smiles. Questions such as "How much is this going to cost?" "How much will my insurance cover?" are, too often, answered with "You mustn't worry about those little things." (I often wondered why they didn't shake their fingers at me during that last one.)

The harsh reality exists, though, that the financial facts of life of a mastectomy woman can mean many shattered hopes and dreams, such as eagerly anticipated vacations, a new car, a quality stereo set for a music lover, or a child's college tuition. When a middle-income patient, then, is "cheered up" by the mastectomy mystique people with gems of wisdom on how important it is for her morale to take a wonderful jaunt to Europe, or to go out and buy herself a beautiful, brand-new wardrobe, is it a wonder that her depression can hit a new low?

Even if a woman's top priority is *not* "Will he continue to find me sexually attractive?" the threat to her sense of womanhood is overwhelming. Helpful hints regarding resumption of sexual relations ("You can resume any time, dear") can only spark further feelings of indignation and outrage, especially for the woman who regarded sex as a total-body (as well as a total-person) experience. For many, this suggestion is about as appealing as having sexual relations while in traction.

The obsession with the prosthesis serving as negation to the entire experience, as far as I'm concerned, has schizophrenic overtones. For the woman whose breasts had as much emotional significance to her as her left large toenail, the theory may have some validity. But for the woman whose breasts were a meaningful aspect of her total sexual experience, this is nothing short of sadistic. To regard ourselves as imitation two-breasted women rather than fully functioning women with one breast (or no breasts) is as dangerous emotionally as inadequate care would be physically.

The matter of facing the scar is another area where the soothing syrup can only make one gag. "You mustn't think of yourself as mutilated—think of what a wonderful person you are" ought to be outlawed. For those of us who've never had surgery other than the mastectomy, the scar is not only a hideous reminder that we once had a living, feeling breast, but that we had expected a scar to look like all the other scars we have seen on hundreds of people—an almost unnoticeable line. The fact that, often, for the first time in our lives, we are faced with a scar that is not *an aspect* of a part of us, but exists *in place* of a part of us, can only add bitterness to existing depression.

A scar can range from a simple diagonal line from the armpit to the center of the chest, as in a modified radical, to a line starting at the upper arm, through the chest, and down the center of the midriff, as in the case of a Halsted radical. It is not so much the shape of the scar that is upsetting as it is the discoloration, rawness, and black threads (which will, of course, eventually be removed) that can remind us of some prehistoric monster.

Recognition has been given to the reality of postpartum depression, and women are, by and large, prepared for it. But for the inevitable depression and anger following a mastectomy, without even the saving grace of having brought a new life into this world, we are only chucked under the chin and treated like darling but overly-precocious children who must, at all costs, be protected from the lurking evil of reality.

Probably, never before in your life have you been surrounded by so many solicitous, well-meaning friends and relatives. As a result, never have you felt that there were so many taboos on thoughts and self-expression. Too often, as a result of the mastectomy friends seem to have turned into smiling robots spewing forth prerecorded announcements of meaningless reassurance coupled with the feeling that you too have turned into a robot, spewing forth messages to the effect that you are "Just fine, thanks" but living in paralyzing terror that you will present an image of anything but "making a wonderful adjustment."

Add to the emotional strain the physical discomfort of never being able to relax, feeling clumsy with the catheters and bandages, not even having the luxury of a bath or shower or being able to spread out in your favorite position in bed to comfort yourself after a trying experience. And what about the woman with small children who has to run a home as though nothing happened, on top of dealing with the children's anxieties of "Mommy, are you going to be all right?"

Is it any wonder that the next time someone tells you how wonderfully you're doing or assures you that you mustn't worry, you'll be tempted to respond with: "One more pep talk and I'll scream"?

However infuriating those pep talks might seem, and however intense the subsequent scream, there will, at some point, be a clearing in the woods.

5
A Clearing in the Woods

No one knows when it will happen or what will bring it about. But just as at one point the world seemed to crash around you after the surgery, at another point there will, somehow, come the realization that maybe things aren't all that bad, anyway.

It could happen when those straitjacket bandages are removed and you have only the lighter bandages covering the incision. It could happen when the incision stops looking like a horror movie close-up and starts to look like any other scar you've ever seen. It could happen when you wake up one morning and realize that you've had a full night's sleep. (That was the one I couldn't believe.) Even if your arm doesn't go straight up over your head, at some point you will have regained most of your original motion. If you've been doing some body exercises as well, you will have become aware that your body will be your own again—not merely an appendage to your operative arm.

By this time, you've gotten back into some sort of routine to carry you through the duration of your recovery. Whether you live alone or with another adult or have a family, you are managing at home and, one hopes, realize that a few specks of dust will simply have to wait. If you go to work, you may have started in gradually on the job. If not, you've probably been in touch with some co-workers, so that you feel you are part of what's going on.

Even if you're not yet able to take a full-fledged shower, at least you can get into a little more than three inches of water in the tub, making sure not to get the bandages wet, if you've still got them on. Even though you've made a lot of progress with your arm, this is no time to rest on your laurels. Whether you're still continuing some of the exercises under your doctor's supervision or have graduated to slow, even motion in doing housework with the arm raised, this is no time to let up on the exercises you still need. Ideally, you have been able to enroll in a community-sponsored post-mastectomy exercise program. Remember, in all progress involving exercises, slow and steady wins the race. The tendency to ignore the rest of the body because of the discomfort in the operative area is one that has to be counteracted. This is a good time to give a little more attention to the balance exercises (see chapter 13), still resting your hands on a stable piece of furniture.

With the confining bandages off, you can look in your closet, and even some store windows, and have some idea of the kind of clothes you'll be able to wear again—probably 98 percent of the styles you wore before. Besides your wide-sleeved shirts, you may be changing off with some of your preop clothes and, except for the ones that may require complicated arm maneuvering, you have a much wider choice now. The nightgowns and lounging robes you wore in the hospital will serve you well at home, too.

If you were able to face your feelings of grief, rage, and fury during your gloomiest moments, the more positive feelings will have a chance to break through. If you've traded in the "cheer up and smile" philosophy for a realistic appraisal of what you're going through, which is a very real sense of loss of something that was precious to you, it will be easier to come to terms with what has happened. Up until now, your time, effort, and thoughts have been occupied with the immediate, near-mechanical motions of getting things together: manipulating your clothes, attending to personal care and household tasks, visiting the doctor, and resuming social schedules. Added to the shock and devastation of having gone through an experience for which you were totally unprepared, you may have gotten the feeling that you had to turn yourself into a robot just to be able to function minimally.

As we discussed in the previous chapter, well-meaning friends and relatives, no matter how altruistic their motives, seem to have a built-in mechanism, if not a downright compulsion, to cheer up or distract anyone who is undergoing any form of despondency or sadness, whatever the cause. We also have to remind ourselves of our reactions when the shoe was on the other foot and we, too, often felt helpless and at a loss for the right thing to say and the right thing to do.

On top of this, most of us have been brought up never to give in to our feelings, never to feel sorry for ourselves or look at the gloomy side of things. If the "think positively" command that is applied to our own health and well-being were extended to every aspect of our lives, no one would ever carry fire insurance or own a pencil with an eraser! It is the "stiff upper lip" attitude in times of stress that can put us into emotional straitjackets. It is the bottled-up resentment that is the forerunner of self-pity, *not* the ability to confront our own feelings—*all* of them!

Many of us have become resentful toward the emotional soothing syrup, which, in some degree, is given to everyone who has undergone a serious illness or accident. Well-meant and, sometimes, not so well-meant cluckings of "What a terrible thing to happen to a wonderful person like you" when we are trying to display a degree of self-sufficiency can only increase our feelings of guilt. We don't feel entitled to our resentment.

If you've had the opportunity and the self-preserving instinct to let your intellect take a back seat and let your emotions take over once in a while, the clearing in the woods will have become apparent that much earlier. Crying, kicking, screaming, and just plain, ordinary swearing, as well as punching a large pillow, will get these emotions exactly where they belong—namely, out of you. And if you do some of that punching with the operative arm, you get an added benefit. Emotions turned inward can become as malignant as runaway cells. And they cannot be removed by surgery, either.

When the concrete wall of rage and fury begins to crumble, then it is time for the emotions that we weren't allowed to admit—even to ourselves—to make their appearance. Sadness, loss, and a sense of mourning will be apparent. The loss of a body part can be as traumatic as the loss of a loved one, but our culture does not, as yet, provide for any period of mourning under these circumstances. Although in all honesty we are entitled to at least as much expression of grief as someone who has lost a loved one, we certainly don't feel a right to be able to share it. Since the day we entered the hospital, people have been looking at us intently searching for a sign of cheerfulness and good spirits as carefully as a doctor listens to a stethoscope for a heartbeat. We feel we owe them a chirpy remark as we owed them thank-you's for the cards and flowers. Those who care for us want to see a sign of how well we're adjusting, or whether we've accepted the loss of a breast. But it is hardly likely that anyone can be expected to accept the fact, at this point; acknowledging the loss is, I believe, more appropriate.

As in the case of any loss, sadness and grief are felt. If this grief can be expressed through crying, either alone or with someone close to you who has an unusual degree of understanding, it can go a long way in cutting through the underbrush. It has been said that we live in a culture where men are permitted to show anger but not to cry, while women are permitted to cry but not to show anger. Our cultural obsession with "keeping our cool" being what it is, too many women feel they don't have the right to cry, either—especially the woman who feels that her image dictates her every word and action.

It is precisely during this period of grief and sadness that the soap-opera syndrome hastens to assure us that we will receive all manner of loving support from husbands (and, in deference to changing life-styles, men who may not be our husbands). The refrain, "Your husband [or lover] will continue to find you attractive" is, unfortunately, sung far too often.

The husbands or other men in our lives are wrestling with their own emotions. Remember, they are as unprepared as we were. Like us, they get caught up in the "should" and "ought to" syndromes and seem to turn into human tape recorders, assuring us that they couldn't care less about the fact that we have lost a breast (or two), in much the same way that we feel we have to assure everyone that everything is "just fine, thanks."

Consequently, expressions of pent-up anger and grief in the presence of a husband are likely to result in increasing doses of reassurances that nothing has changed. And the more genuinely concerned the husband or lover, the louder will be the protestations that the mastectomy makes no difference to him. This, in turn, can only increase the feeling that we have to put on a good show, especially when we are sensitive to the fact that he is making such an effort on our behalf.

If you have a close friend (and, yes, a husband can fall into this category) in whose presence you can express grief and sadness without fear of receiving protestations and assurances that "it isn't so," you have a rare friend and, by all means, share your feelings with him or her. Otherwise, arrange to have some time alone during which you can close a door and not fear that you will be "caught in the act."

Part of the old cliché, "Cry and you cry alone," is going to have to be reevaluated. We do many things alone. We take care of personal body functions alone. We read alone. We wash and dress alone. Are these actions to be condemned because we do them alone? Or should our first priority be that they have to be done and that we could not function as human beings if they were not done—alone or otherwise? There are times when we need to cry, just as there are times when our bodies need to rid themselves of waste matter. Try to dam up either function and you're asking for trouble—physical or emotional, and often, both.

One good cry is not going to transform any primitive jungle into a well-manicured lawn. It will, however, go a long way in providing that clearing in the woods. In that clearing you will be able to see, perhaps dimly at first, the outline of a future and the image of a new you or a slightly altered version of the former you. This could be a time to rebuild: a revitalized body, a revitalized outlook, a revitalized human being.

You've already gained something as a result of the mastectomy—the ability to face facts and feelings head on.

There's a certain strength to be found ahead when fears and terror are behind you.

6
Facts and Fiction

After the clearing in the woods, there is usually the ability, or more accurately, the willingness, to face facts that we were unwilling or unable to face before.

By this time, we've learned that the dread and horror preceding the surgery itself was, by and large, unjustified. As unprepared as we may have been for the surgery and the ability to cope with attendant problems of recovery, most of us are even less prepared to cope with attitudes and mystiques surrounding the entire subject of mastectomies.

Of the entire spectrum of what is loosely known as women's troubles, breast cancer is the only one that is damaged more by *new* wives' tales than the time-honored old ones, from which no item pertaining to female anatomy can ever fully escape. The old wives' tales surrounding mastectomies were a cross between fairy tales and Gothic horror stories, and they are still with us. This is the bedrock of the bleeding heart syndrome surrounding breast cancer—a syndrome made up of tales ranging from undying love on the part of the husband of a mastectomy patient to cancer (in any form) being a contagious disease.

Just as we were emerging from the Dark Ages of the bleeding heart syndrome, we seemed to enter the Age of Enlightenment whose founding mothers were, by and large, composed of the more militant segment of the women's liberation movement. This new awareness, however, gave rise to something equally dangerous and appalling, the clenched fist syndrome. According to this new complication, the cure was worse than the disease itself and, along with every evil in this world, the blame for breast cancer and mastectomies could be laid at the door of the true culprits—men. It is, unfortunately, the clenched fist syndrome that has done more to spread the gospel of misinformation regarding successful treatment of breast cancer through the mass media than the bleeding heart syndrome has been able to do about *their* misinformation since the first Mesopotamian woman leaned over her back fence to assure her neighbor that the "black bile" was the cause of breast cancer.

Bleeding heart or clenched fist, whatever the source of the misinformation, myths are going to have to be replaced by reality if any woman wants to give herself a fair chance of either getting competent medical care of adjusting to the facts of mastectomy life. Let's tackle each of these myths, one at a time. They are presented here in no particular order.

"Your husband will give you unlimited, loving support" is probably highest on the list of the soap opera proponents. As in the case of any marriage with strong emotional foundations, a period of crisis will create an even closer intimacy than before, which is the reason that so many women have honestly reported improved sexual relations following a mastectomy. But can we deny the fact that the divorce rate in the United States is approaching a one-in-three ratio? A problem marriage is simply not going to be strengthened by any personal upheaval. And what about the man who is, himself, in need of loving support? The loss of a breast does not, or should not, mean the loss of our ability to understand the problems and anxieties of those closest to us. Divorces *do* occur, but it is highly unlikely that a mastectomy (or any other personal crisis) could shake the foundations of a truly secure marriage.

"You're the same wonderful person you always were" has long been another of my favorites. Along with undying devotion on the part of a husband, this mystique would lead us to believe that breast cancer is limited to wonderful women with loving husbands only. If so, do nasty, unmarried women have a built-in immunity against breast cancer?

As to being the same person you always were, very few people could undergo such a traumatic experience without its leaving some effect on them. I am not the same person I was prior to my mastectomy (and the consensus among my friends is that it might just be a good thing!).

"Only a woman who has had a mastectomy can understand the problems of another mastectomy woman" is another common myth associated with the bleeding heart syndrome. The adjustment problems surrounding a mastectomy are not the same for the thirty-year-old mother of three, feeding her family on a tight budget, as they are for a wealthy widow of seventy. No one would dream of applying instant sisterhood to two women who had just given birth, if one of these women was comfortably middle class and had planned for a child and the other already had more children than she could afford and whose husband had left her during her pregnancy. But no one hesitates in comparing us with aunts, cousins, and diverse socialites whose life-styles differ so radically from our own. To underestimate the ability to understand and share problems on the part of our own non-mastectomy friends, as well as the professionals in various fields who are eager to help post-mastectomy women in adjusting to life, is to underestimate ourselves as well as others.

"Sexual relations should resume as soon as possible" is another favorite maxim of the bleeding heart syndrome, and I say it's fine for any woman whose sexuality has been a study in still life. This is in the same category as a friendly tip I received from a woman I know whose friend underwent a mastectomy. "Always make love with your brassiere and prosthesis on—my friend does." Such advice is actually a disservice to a man as well as a woman. The denial of reality can only create emotional obstacles, which, in turn, create obstacles to every aspect of the intimate relationship.

"We live in a breast-oriented society." I'd like to modify this one, somewhat. We live in a surface-appearance-oriented society, and mechanized, plasticized, air-brushed substitutes are idolized by men with potency problems. Granted, large breasts are a feature of this hybrid. But if emphasis were placed on large breasts alone, centerfolds of the girlie magazines would probably be adorned with photographs of 300-pound women. Women want to be attractive and loved and admired for themselves. But when one part of the body is isolated, and emotionally disturbed men become obsessed by that one body part, we can hardly regard it as flattering.

For emotionally disturbed men to create an image of women

based on plasticized appurtenances rather than human feeling is indicative of *their* problems. For a woman to attempt to fit into that image is indicative of *her* problem.

A woman who has undergone a mastectomy will no longer be regarded as a "sex object" by men who regard women as sex objects. Fat chance!

The lumpectomy is a viable alternative to a radical mastectomy. The chief proponent of this myth has already rejected it. (See chapter 18, "Family and Social Relationships.") However, the clenched fist brigade is still militantly standing up for its beliefs.

"A woman should be allowed to have a lumpectomy or anything else she wants, even if her surgeon disapproves" is a tactic that was discarded along with bra-burning. Not so. It is the message of a book on breast cancer published in 1975 (A.D.).*

A woman who has had a mastectomy should automatically see a psychiatrist. Many post-mastectomy women could benefit from some form of emotional therapy, either because of problems resulting from the mastectomy or because of preexisting problems. (This subject is discussed more fully in chapter 9, "Deeper than the Scar.") However, before we automatically prescribe psychiatric care for all post-mastectomy women, some sort of research will have to be done so that we may have statistics on the number of women who have developed breast cancer *after* a number of years of psychiatric treatment. From a branch of the medical profession that has consistently refused to make data available as to the results of their treatment, this is not a likely probability in the foreseeable future.

Bleeding heart or clenched fist; old wives' tales or new wives' tales—the foregoing represent only a few of the myths with which a post-mastectomy woman has to cope. Attitudes *do* change toward us, as do our attitudes toward ourselves and, consequently, our attitudes ·toward others. We cannot pretend that there is no stigma attached to the word *cancer*. Job prejudice does exist; people *can* burst into tears when they first see us after surgery; and the young and attractive woman *will* overhear "boob" jokes, some of them intentional.

We are not the only people who ever have had to undergo a

*Rose Kushner, *Breast Cancer: A Personal History and an Investigative Report* (New York: Harcourt Brace Jovanovich, 1975), p. 194.

personal crisis. To a large degree, our predicament can be likened to the successful executive who suddenly has been fired. He cannot help but be aware of changed attitudes toward him and, consequently, a changed attitude toward himself. Like the recently fired executive, we are going through a trial by fire. We've pulled through the surgery only to be answered by musty clichés when we searched for human understanding. In seeking competent medical help, we opted for life. It is hoped we will all opt to live that life to the fullest. We are at a crossroad, and it can be frightening. We've paid for our life with a breast. We may have to pay for the quality of that life by smashing a few icons, and, possibly, a few relationships. We had to face an unfortunate reality when we faced the word *malignancy*. We will have to face a few more unfortunate realities where our social adjustment is concerned.

One of those unfortunate realities, and one that is *not* limited to women who have undergone mastectomies, is that people are forgiven their failures far more readily than they are forgiven their triumphs. People are loved more readily for their weaknesses than for their strengths. There is nothing quite like a catastrophic illness to set the emotional vultures salivating, unless it is an unhappy love affair. Some people are so structured that their illusion of self-worth is in direct proportion to the pity they can wring out of themselves on behalf of others. Under the guise of concern for our welfare, their morbid curiosity can be more emotionally draining than the surgery itself. Those who offer themselves up as handy hate targets aren't doing us any favors, either.

If you're reasonably attractive, there may be other women who will secretly (or not so secretly) enjoy seeing you taken down a peg or two. (Wait till they see you *rise* a peg or two!) While our culture can cheer the loving wife/homemaker who smiles through her tears as she raises her operative arm toward well-wishers, the single, independent woman who is determined to fight her way back to her preop condition (or better) is not going to be greeted by quite so many cheers from those who feel threatened by her.

Close to a million women who have undergone mastectomies are leading active, enriched lives. Many of these women have openly announced the fact and have done much to bring the word *mastectomy* out of the closet. Other women in the public eye have chosen to keep this aspect of their lives quiet. How many of us would ever guess that the opera singer or prima ballerina once had to face the shock of seeing the scar for the first time? How many of us would guess that the beautiful young woman we saw walking on the beach; the long-haired mod girl in her patched jeans, attending a poetry reading with her bearded lover, had ever been tormented by the doubt that she might be repulsive to a man?

It is because most of these women choose not to announce their mastectomies that we have become "the woman without an image" or, worse still, the woman whose image has been so grotesquely distorted by the mass media. Between being treated on the one hand like poor, precious darlings who must be petted constantly and on the other hand as victims of a sadistic, mercenary medical profession, is it any wonder that we feel we've been placed in limbo?

Have I painted a picture of unmitigated doom? To assume that every committed relationship will be shattered, every friendship will cool, every woman you encounter will chide you condescendingly for having had a mastectomy, every neighbor will take a sadistic delight in feeling sorry for you, is as destructive and unrealistic as expecting a path strewn with rose petals. Whether or not any of these things will happen, to pretend the possibility does not exist is like trying to pretend that breast cancer does not exit. Self-delusion or delusion from others is a luxury we cannot afford.

Fairy tales or Gothic horror stories—they have to be destroyed. And when myths are destroyed there is usually a lot of rubble. We will hear cries of "Ingratitude!" from both the bleeding hearts and the clenched fists.

But it's the first step in the process of rebuilding.

7

Facing Our Deepest Fears

Under ordinary circumstances, if a woman were to discuss the advisability of making out a will, she would be regarded as sensible, level-headed, and able to face reality. However, when a woman who has recently undergone a mastectomy tries to discuss that very same question, she is likely to face horrified denials from her friends. Just as she was not allowed to consider the possibility of the mastectomy itself, once again she is forbidden to think about the one eventuality that will happen to every human being.

Like any doubt or anxiety that cannot find expression through open, honest communication, these forbidden thoughts can only fester inside to create additional problems. When the word *cancer* is involved, for many people, the major dread is not so much "Am I going to die?" as it is "Will I be forced to have a meaningless, painful, and empty life prolonged unnecessarily?" This is the question that thunders so loudly within when one is afraid to express it.

Fortunately, there are professional individuals and organizations who understand the priority of these matters, and discussion with them can result in calm assessment of the situation rather than frenzied hysteria.

Thanks to the efforts of the Euthanasia Society, there is a growing awareness in medical circles of the need for a patient to express these anxieties without receiving evasive murmurs. Dr.

Elisabeth Kubler-Ross, in her excellent book, *Questions and Answers on Death and Dying*, tackles this subject honestly, forth-rightly, and humanely. The ability to discuss these questions openly with your doctor could be one of the most confidence-building aspects of your relationship with him or her. Even if a doctor's answer is "Frankly, I don't know," we can, at least, feel that a straightforward answer, and not a patronizing, placating one, has been obtained.

We have all heard of people—young or old, sick or healthy—dying suddenly without having left a will. Even if the person were not the family breadwinner, the hardships that those closest to the deceased had to undergo only added tragedy to a basically unhappy situation. While many people automatically carry some form of life insurance, most people have a tendency to regard a will as something they have plenty of time for later—preferably as they are approaching ninety.

For a calm, rational opinion on the subject of a woman and a will, I went to Camille S. LoCurto, vice-president/controller of the First Women's Bank in New York City. Her reaction was that *every person* should have a will.

Many of us regard a will as something involving lawyers and vast wealth, but a will is at least as essential to the person of limited means as it is to the property owner. Ms. LoCurto also pointed out that, as none of us can predict the day when we will draw our last breath, neither can we predict the circumstances. We have the same chance of getting involved in a fatal accident that anyone else has. This may involve litigation, making your estate worth far more than you could imagine.

For the woman whose property includes stocks, bonds, and real estate, the services of an attorney are called for. Most financial questions can be answered by an officer of your bank. There are many competent practicing lawyers in every state, and a woman might feel more comfortable discussing this traditionally male bastion subject with an informed, qualified woman practitioner. But, as in the selection of a gynecologist, competence and proper rapport should be important considerations.

It was Ms. LoCurto who pointed out the special needs of a woman living alone and the usefulness of her appointing a custodian—someone to whom you will give power of attorney in the event that you may be in a state where you are unable to make your own decisions, such as being hospitalized due to an accident or any other situation. The person in whom you invest power of attorney will be able to take care of your financial and legal matters, such as dealing with insurance companies so that your needs will be met. Choosing such a person, and the conditions under which he or she may be able to act on your behalf (such as unconsciousness or heavy sedation), can be discussed beforehand with an officer of your bank.

An individual will is as necessary to a married woman dependent on her husband for financial support as it is to a single woman. If you want to broach this subject to your husband, you might point out tax burdens that may be imposed because of the lack of a will. Your attorney will be in a position to advise you on matters such as joint ownership of property.

For many people, the quality of life takes precedence over the quantity of life, and these people are especially concerned about being kept alive technically, when they may no longer be active participants in the process of life itself. As a result of this concern, the Euthanasia Society, which is popular among growing numbers of people today, was formed in 1938 to deal with the legal aspects of the question. In order to make the public aware of its aims, the Euthanasia Educational Council was started in 1967, and their "Living Will" has done much not only to make the most "unmentionable" topic of our culture mentionable, but also to create an awareness that human beings are entitled to at least as much humane treatement at life's decline as are household pets. The document states:

> If the situation should arise in which there is no reasonable expectation of my recovery from physical or mental disability, I request that I be allowed to die and not be kept alive by artificial means or "heroic measures." I do not fear death itself as much as the indignities of deterioration, dependence and hopeless pain. I, therefore, ask that medication be mercifully administered to me to alleviate suffering even though this may hasten the moment of death.

Although the Living Will is not a *legally binding* document, neither can it be called an illegal document. It is not legally binding because no precedent ever has been set for its use. Currently, legislation is pending in fifteen states to make it legally binding.

The Patient's Bill of Rights is a twelve-point document developed by the American Hospital Association. Its basic thesis is that the patient has the right to be informed and consulted as to forms of treatment, as well as the right to a say in the decisions as to the circumstances when life should or should not be sustained.

Many patients who have signed the Living Will present it to the hospital upon admission, where it is included in the patient's records as a statement of the patient's desires and beliefs.

A copy of the Living Will, as well as a Patient's Bill of Rights and answers to questions most frequently asked about the subject of euthanasia, is available on request by writing to:

Euthanasia Educational Council
250 West 57th Street
New York, New York 10019

The Council reports that many doctors are becoming more amenable to discussing the Living Will with their patients and that many patients, on entering a hospital, submit a copy of it to be entered with their charts.

No matter what their age or status of their health, many people have found that having a signed and notarized copy of the Living Will in their possession is often helpful in breaking the ice with close members of the family. Remember, the Living Will can do as much for your peace of mind as a regular will can. And as so many hundreds of thousands of people have found out, instead of being synonymous with depression and morbidity, the Living Will has become the affirmation of "the will to live."

Once you have made some positive effort in preparing for *any* unforeseen emergency, whether a sprained ankle or a fatal plane crash, you will be in a better position to discuss the subject openly with a close friend or relative. The next time you hear an indignant "But you mustn't *think* of such a thing!" you will be able to answer, quietly and calmly, "I wasn't thinking of a recurrence. I was thinking about an ordinary accident that can and does happen to a healthy, vigorous person in the prime of life."

There will be a feeling of breathing easier once this has been accomplished, not only on your part, but for those close to you, as well.

Death in itself is not a tragedy. The fear of facing the reality of death is the tragedy, as it is inevitably accompanied by the fear of facing the reality of life.

8
Related Health Matters

During the period immediately following surgery, your primary health concern will be related to the surgery itself. You are probably aware that you will have to go for regular checkups for the rest of your life. A great deal of emphasis has been placed on self-examination following surgery, both on the remaining breast and on the scar area. Your doctor will advise you on this. If your tendency is to be cystic, your doctor will instruct you as to your best method of self-examination.

During visits to your doctor's office, you will be surrounded by other women in the waiting room who are there for the same reason you are. There is a comforting feeling about being among those who are in the same boat. However, the tendency to compare notes with other women who are under the care of your doctor, as well as with women who have undergone mastectomies with other surgeons, is one that it is wiser to avoid. The healing process is an individual one, and the surgery performed on you is not exactly the same as it was for the woman sitting in the chair opposite you. Patients vary in their need for postoperative radiation treatments or chemotherapy. The fact that your treatment differs from another woman's does not mean you are being either cheated or overtreated. To compare your case with someone else's is every bit as foolhardy as taking medication prescribed for someone else. There are probably no two mastectomies that are exactly alike. In order to obtain a good picture of your own specific case, you might want to ask your doctor about the following subjects:

• Procedure for self-examination following surgery
• Restrictions on contraceptives
• Advisability of preganancy and breast-feeding
• Restrictions on estrogen or other hormone therapy relating to menopause
• Advice on douching

The fact that you have undergone a mastectomy does not mean that you are faced with a life of semi-invalidism or a need for picky attention to petty details. However, you will want to give serious thought to every aspect of your general health—a subject to which *everyone* should give serious thought. Because of the mastectomy, we tend to become preoccupied with the arm area only, fully losing sight of the fact that sufficient rest, exercise, diet, and general health habits (which are discussed more fully elsewhere) are equally necessary. We are no more immune to colds, flue, viruses, or petty aches and pains than is the general population. We do, however, have more motivation for keeping ourselves in good condition in order to minimize minor illnesses.* We are probably in a position to appreciate good health and a well-functioning body as we never have been before.

In the field of medicine today, the family doctor or general practitioner is no longer the one person who handles all your medical needs. Besides your surgeon, there may be other physicians whom you will be seeing, but because of the mastectomy it is quite important that these other doctors do not prescribe any form of treatment that would be contraindicated by the mastectomy. If your surgeon was recommended to you by your internist or general practitioner, you can be sure that there will be open communication from one to another as far as your future medical needs are concerned. One area of medical care that will have to receive serious attention following a mastectomy is gynecological care. In fact, this may become your second-highest medical priority, assuming you have no other major health problems. If, prior to the surgery, a gynecologist was someone you visited for a Pap test (a

---

*The major function of the lymph glands is to fight infection. With lymph nodes possibly removed during mastectomy, we must be extra careful about infections of any type.

test for cancer of the uterus) whenever you thought about it (which probably wasn't too often, anyway), a change in thinking (and action) is going to have to come about. While every woman is advised to have a Pap test and thorough gynecological examination once a year, for women over thirty-five and women of any age who have had mastectomies, twice a year is becoming the general rule.

It is my own belief that the choice of a gynecologist is one of the most crucial professional relationships a woman can form, and one where the emotional factor must be taken into consideration at least as much as the doctor's credentials. Especially after having lost a breast, the first and foremost priority in choosing a gynecologist is a sense of being respected both as a human being and as a woman. Much has been said about the condescending attitude of gynecologists (indicating men) toward their patients. For too many women, a visit to the gynecologist has been an ordeal to be endured rather than an intelligent discussion between two adults. The pat-on-the-head attitude that has characterized too many gynecologist/patient relationships has, rightly, been denounced by factions of the women's movement. *The New Woman's Survival Sourcebook* contains the news:

> Carol Downer, Lorraine Rothman, and the Feminist Women's Health Center women of Los Angeles, for the most part non-professional laywomen, released women from thousands of years of subjugation with the simple but radical ideas of gynecological self-help which encompass vaginal self-examination and menstrual extraction.*

In too many cases, however, the solution to this problem has been more damaging than the problem itself. The do-it-yourself trend in gynecology that has been fostered by the feminists has brought sharp criticism from leading practitioners, *including* women doctors. A self-styled "clinic" in Boston was, fortunately, closed when it became known that "sisters" had been treating one another's vaginal infections with local applications of yogurt.

As important as the interpersonal relationship with a gynecologist is for *any* woman, for the post-mastectomy woman another factor must be taken into consideration, and that is the gynecologist's relationship to the breast surgeon. If the gynecologist

*Lolly Hirsch, "Practicing Health Without a License," from *The New Woman's Survival Sourcebook* (New York: Alfred A. Knopf, 1975) p. 33.

was recommended by the surgeon or vice versa, they are probably in general agreement. If, however, the surgeon is not professionally associated with the gynecologist, each must be aware of the other's stand on one crucial matter—estrogen. The question of estrogen will arise in three instances: the contraceptive pill; estrogen therapy during menopause; and pregnancy. In the first two instances, estrogen will be introduced by an outside source; in the last, the estrogen will be produced by the body itself, usually doubling the normal body output.

Although the relationship of estrogen and breast cancer has been established and agreed upon among gynecologists and oncologists, it is only recently that estrogen treatment has been linked with rising uterine cancer rates among the menopausal and post-menopausal patients receiving the treatment. While no definite causal relationship has been proven, studies are currently under way to determine why the uterine cancer rates are five to fourteen times higher in women who receive estrogen treatment than in women who do not.

I have asked Dr. Michael Truppin, attending obstetrician-gynecologist at Mount Sinai Hospital in New York, for his opinions regarding both general gynecological care and the gynecologist/surgeon relationship. Dr. Truppin emphasized the point that where there was a variance of opinion between the two, a consultation is indicated and, if necessary, should be demanded by the patient. Although estrogen treatment is generally ruled out for post-mastectomy patients, Dr. Truppin believes that, depending on the extent of the mastectomy after a minimum of two years has passed, and other factors relating to the patient's history, small amounts of estrogen may be safely prescribed. He hastens to point out that this treatment must meet with the approval of the surgeon as well.

Although post-mastectomy women were once soothingly reassured that they ran no higher risk of complications if they wanted to have children than did non-mastectomy women, recent findings have changed this belief. Most patients are advised against pregnancy. Once again, this is an individual question, and your surgeon's opinion should be sought in this matter. The same is true for breast-feeding.

Ideas on douching, if at all, and what solutions to use, vary according to the opinions of individual gynecologists, and a woman should discuss these with her gynecologist rather than her neighbor. But, like every other ethical practitioner in the field, Dr. Truppin takes a strong stand on vaginal "cosmetics"—perfumed douches, sprays, and other chemical preparations—and that stand is firmly against. These products have caused serious irritation and infection, and Dr. Truppin believes, as do his colleagues, that they should be removed from the market or at least carry a warning label.

If a woman has a tendency toward bacterial or fungal infection, constrictive clothing, such as body suits, panty hose, tight slacks, and tampons, in some cases, should be avoided. Even for the average woman, tight slacks on top of body suits on top of panty hose, worn every day, interfere with proper ventilation and can eventually cause discomfort and problems. For the woman who does not like the idea of wearing a girdle, garter belts and regular hose are again becoming readily available in stores.

The question of contraceptives for the post-mastectomy woman is discussed in chapter 17. However, I will say here that your surgeon should be aware of the method you are using and, if you are contemplating a change, it should be discussed with your surgeon as well as your gynecologist.

The general health picture covers more than regular visits to various doctors and following their advice. This could prove to be an ideal time to revise a passive attitude toward health—diet, exercise, rest, and leisure—in sum, a total way of thinking and living.

Medically, no one will ever take chances with a post-mastectomy woman. The slightest suspicion that something may be wrong can mean a battery of tests and examinations. This is unquestionably annoying, but at least we know that no stone is being left unturned where our health is concerned. Sooner or later the realization will sink in that we have a better outlook regarding the all-around health picture than our more fortunate acquaintances who have never had to face a major illness.

9
Deeper than the Scar

Ever since the expression *psychosomatic illness* became part of the medical (and general) vocabulary, it has been common knowledge that certain illnesses can be emotional in origin. While the word *psychosomatic* was originally reserved for ulcers and later for hypertension, it was used rather liberally in describing vague, unspecified disorders such as headaches, backaches, colds, and flu. The word itself carried the hint of hypochondria rather than any organic disorder.

Although it later became acceptable to correlate emotional disturbances with other, more serious illnesses, for some reason, the word *cancer* received diplomatic immunity from any connection with the word *neurotic*. A neurotic person was one who could display physiological symptoms with no organic basis, and it was generally thought that these psychosomatic fears served as some sort of guarantee that the neurotic would never have a "real" illness. Cancer, especially, was the one disease that the orthodox Freudians condescendingly exempted from the cure-all catch phrases of psychiatric jargon.

As we are fortunate in living in an era in which advanced medical discoveries make a cure for cancer a reality in an increasingly high number of cases, so are we fortunate in being on the threshold of discoveries of the relationship between cancer and preexisting emotional disorder, to the extent that emotional therapy has resulted in prolonging *meaningful* and *active* life in patients formerly considered terminal. This perceptive and dynamic work is being led by a few pioneers in the field. One of those pioneers is Clelia Goodyear, a practicing New York psychotherapist who became interested in the problems of terminal cancer patients and their families and whose efforts have resulted in remissions undreamed of as recently as two years ago. While the problems of a recent post-mastectomy woman cannot be compared to those faced by people whose illness is so far advanced, Ms. Goodyear feels that special services are needed for the post-mastectomy woman as well (even though, in most cases, our prognoses are termed "excellent"), and she is active in organizing leaders in the medical field for an awareness of our needs.

Even if a woman could have been graded A-plus in emotional health prior to a mastectomy, the experience alone could test the psychic endurance of an emotional Lady Samson. Because of the emotional crucifixion most of us underwent from the first visit to the surgeon until we woke up in the recovery room, the battle for human dignity far eclipsed the battle for the breast. This applies equally to the woman who was given the all clear after the biopsy and to the woman who has had a bilateral mastectomy.

Because most of our friends and relatives (along with quite a few members of the medical and psychiatric profession) cannot face a word that traditionally has been associated with fatality, we can sometimes feel that, as our surface adjustment improves, the emotional jungle is thrown proportionately into deeper turmoil. For many people the thought of seeking psychological help for their problems could, in itself, be a trauma. But the experience of being treated progressively as more of a thing and less of a human being can take its emotional toll even on those of us whose physical recovery can be described as amazing. The dehumanizing process of superclinical efficiency combined with the alienating response we have received when we tried to express our feelings can often lead to a self-image of "non-person," in addition to doubts many of us have had about being a "non-woman."

An emotionally and financially secure woman who has received red carpet treatment in the hospital is in a better position to withstand the psychic damage than is the lower or middle-income level woman who has, too often, been treated as some sort of derelict. The medical profession is creating additional problems for the post-mastectomy woman by refusing to acknowledge the need for *emotional* along with *physical* recovery. Although there are one or two major hospitals that are pioneering programs to cope with the emotional needs of the mastectomy patient, including referral for psychological help when indicated, the needs of the vast majority of women are glossed over with "We must keep a cheerful attitude, mustn't we?"

For the woman whose closest relationships have been based on honest, open expression of fears and anxieties, her friend, husband, or lover may be able to provide the almost superhuman understanding needed to see her through this upheaval (not to mention the problems that person may be undergoing himself as a result of the woman's problems). But for the vast majority of women who feel that they must not burden those closest to them, outside help may be in order.

According to Clelia Goodyear, a woman seeking psychological help following a mastectomy should try to find a therapist and a method of therapy that is most suitable to her particular needs. And Ms. Goodyear is quick to emphasize that the form of therapy should provide for *emotional expression* of fears, anxieties, rage, and terror, rather than merely a verbal description. Anger, rage, and grief must be vented before they are turned inward to create more physical, as well as emotional damage. It is for this reason that Ms. Goodyear considers conventional forms of therapy—long, drawn-out classical analysis—unsuitable and potentially destructive for the post-mastectomy patient. The average orthodox practitioner is simply not equipped, either emotionally or by training, to face the anxieties within himself that will be unearthed by a patient whose illness and problems come under the category of real rather than imagined.

The ENCORE (Encouragement, Normalcy, Counseling, Opportunity, Reaching Out, Energies revived) program of the YWCA, which is a community program for post-mastectomy patients, does provide "rap sessions" as part of their services, but leaders of ENCORE hasten to point out that they are in no way to be regarded as "therapy sessions." ENCORE leaders mention that the camaraderie provided by the program often alleviates a woman's feeling of isolation, but if psychological help is indicated, the individual YWCA will refer the woman to an approved psychological counseling service, where she will be given a choice of therapists equipped to deal with her problem. (See chapter 13 for information regarding membership in ENCORE.) Kristine Burkard conducts a post-mastectomy exercise/swim program at the 92nd Street YM-YWHA in New York City. Although independent of the ENCORE program, this, too, refers women to specialized therapists in this area.

The choice of a therapist as well as the form of therapy is of prime importance and a very individual decision. While group therapy can work out very well for some people, the idea is anathema to others. Second only to that involved in the choice of a gynecologist is the emotional factor essential in establishing a relationship with a therapist. Much has been said and written lately about women therapists being better equipped emotionally to deal with the psychological problems of a woman, especially those related to physical disorders. I cannot go along with this completely. Clelia Goodyear has pointed out that a woman therapist, unless she has been trained or had experience in this area, could come to feel more threatened if she could not face the possibility of this eventuality in her own life.

Fortunately, a woman has her choice today of therapist as well as method of therapy, and there is a much healthier atmosphere being created in thinking of the patient as a consumer rather than as a victim, which was all too prevalent in the early days of psychological treatment.

Barbara Bederson is a therapist with Aura Groups, located at 102 East 30th Street, in New York City. Although its name implies group sessions only, individual sessions are also available. At Aura emphasis is placed on emotional expression and dealing with feelings directly rather than intellectual discussions of the emotions involved. Ms. Bederson is strongly in favor of the patient as the chooser rather than the one decided upon grudgingly by the potential therapist. She feels that the patient has the right to ask questions of the therapist at the outset and, if necessary, to shop around before a commitment is made for therapeutic treatment.

During the course of therapy, a woman will undoubtedly confront problems, feelings, and attitudes which existed long before she ever had the mastectomy and, in many cases, long before she had breasts. These might be problems that have been lying dormant for years which have been triggered off by the mastectomy. In many instances, there can be a tendency to blame the mastectomy for totally unrelated problems. There can be unpleasant facts to face, such as using the mastectomy to escape full responsibility for our own actions and behavior toward others. The overabundance of misguided pity that is showered upon a woman after a mastectomy can, unfortunately, be harvested by a woman to her own ends, often to her detriment.

The thought of seeking psychological help can be more threatening to some women than the thought of the mastectomy itself, and no anesthesia is administered during therapy, either. But for so many people, therapy has been a major step in *total recovery*, not only from a physical illness but from problems that had their roots in the beginnings of their entire lives.

It's only fair to warn you, though: If you decide to tell people about starting therapy, the reactions will be as varied and often horrified as the reactions to the mastectomy itself. "But, darling, there's nothing wrong with you—you're making such a *wonderful* adjustment." "You've been through so much already, why do you have to upset yourself further?" "Why are you convincing yourself that there's something wrong with you mentally?" These are but a few. However, the all-time classic to be guarded against is "But you have *me* to talk to—haven't we always been the best of friends?" Turning to a loving friend with the best intentions as a way of dealing with an emotional disorder is about as wise as turning to a loving friend to perform surgery. There is a vast difference between a friend and a qualified practitioner, in *any* specialty. Let us not confuse the two.

Chapter 20, "Vultures of the Living," deals with the well-intentioned incompetents and outright quacks who peddle miracle cures for cancer (and every other disease from dandruff onward) in the form of drugs, machinery, and diets. At least as much quackery is offered in miracle cures by self-styled mind healers via instant weekends, thought control, and the like. At this writing, there is a miracle weekend fad that promises cures for emotional stress, colds, headaches, major illness and, of course, sexual problems. By the time you read this, its founding father will probably be in jail or in Switzerland, but that doesn't mean there won't be dozens to take his place and promise the miracle that he failed to perform. People who are seeking painless panaceas instead of often painful confrontation with reality are headed for as much heartbreak and tragedy as people seeking "the little pink pill" as a cure-all for physical disorders.

Facing the fact that emotional help is needed may not always be ego-flattering. But as more and more facts are coming to light about the role of emotional therapy as one of the weapons in the arsenal of successfully battling cancer, a little bit of ego-deflation seems to be a pretty small price to pay, doesn't it?

Phase II
REAWAKENING

10
Taking the Bull by the Horns

"A part of me was taken from me and I'm going to put the rest of myself in good shape, dammit!"

That's what I said to myself when I looked in the mirror a few weeks after surgery. I had put on twenty pounds as "insurance" prior to the mastectomy. I had picked up the rumor (false, as most rumors are) that a weight gain or at least the absence of weight loss, represented some sort of guarantee that it could not possibly be cancer. I had been through every petrifying anxiety that anyone goes through before the biopsy. I had seen the change in attitude of those around me. After some fairly rough-and-tumble backslapping, I was suddenly treated with emotional kid gloves. I felt that I had become "someone who has to be watched carefully."

As a young and active woman, I had to face the question, "Do I want to live with only one breast?" From a life that included ice skating and ballet class as a regular part of my activity, I suddenly had to watch every step. Physical activity had been my way of coping with anger and frustration. I became overwhelmed with disgust—disgust for my own body, which I began to regard as a burden, and disgust with my friends, who I felt had failed me.

Let's face it—the loss of a breast was an ego thing with me, as well, as it is for virtually all the younger, unmarried mastectomy women. Reassurances from my lover were not much consolation. I accused him of feeling sorry for me.

Fortunately, in recent years women have been encouraged to pay more attention to their bodies as an expression of their inner selves. Because most of us have found out that wishing won't always make it so in the case of having an ideal body, we have come to realize that some thought and effort have to be employed as well. However, most of us are too defensive to say, "I want a beautiful body," and when complimented on our bodies, we feel compelled to make a self-derogatory remark in the name of the misguided modesty. Although we no longer feel it essential to keep our bodies hidden, we are still a little hesitant about admitting the pride we take in our bodies, for fear of being called arrogant.

Often, following a mastectomy, many of us have had to face for the first time in our lives the most crucial of all our relationships—our relationship to our own bodies. For most of us, our bodies have always been *there* and, by and large, taken very much for granted, in much the way we feel that we, as people, have been taken for granted. Most of us have thought about our bodies in terms of what we didn't like about them—"My hips are too big," "If only I weren't so short-waisted." For most of us, a blushing "I really shouldn't . . ." as we reach for another piece of banana cream pie has been the extent of what we consider to be our responsibility to our own bodies.

According to the mastectomy mystique, we're not only expected to make light of the fact that we've lost a breast, we're expected to regard our entire bodies as something that was never really that important, anyway. Evidently, a renewed interest in needlepoint is supposed to make us a wonderful person, or even more wonderful than we were before the mastectomy. This same mastectomy mystique would have us believe that it is a medically proven fact that mastectomies can be performed on wonderful people only.

Those of us who regarded our breasts as beautiful feel that they have yet another shame to hide. Although no one would condemn a mother for mourning the loss of a beautiful child, few of us feel we would get much sympathy if we verbally regretted the loss of a beautiful breast. Even for those of us who regarded our breasts as not quite comparable to a classic Greek statue's, they were still our passport to womanhood during adolescence. The purchase of that first brassiere told the world that we had arrived—we weren't babies any more.

Who among us has not suffered unexpected pangs of grief long after we felt that we had adjusted to the fact of the mastectomy: stepping out of the shower and trying to dry both breasts, thumbing through a fashion magazine and seeing filmy lingerie, seeing a photograph of yourself in a bathing suit taken years before the mastectomy?

And what weapons do we have to deal with this heartbreak? The mastectomy mystique offers us one thing—denial. We are expected to deny that our bodies had any meaning to us; we are expected to deny the mastectomy itself; most heartbreaking of all, we are expected to deny the fact that a liquid-filled prosthesis is not really an adequate substitute for a lost breast. We are assured that we can fool the world, if only our prosthesis feels like the natural breast.

We are expected to accept the mastectomy. Perhaps it would be more realistic to expect us to become resigned to the fact, at least in the beginning. Even when we have completely acknowledged the fact on a mental or intellectual level, there is a much deeper part of us that tends to make us forget, block out, or make believe it never happened. To swallow the soothing syrup with which the mastectomy mystique tries to force-feed us is asking for trouble. It is only when we realize the full depth of our loss that we can become determined to compensate for that loss.

We are not the only people in the world who have faced shock and devastation. Widowhood has thrown many young women into a state of social leprosy in addition to the very real emotional and financial problems. People have invested their life savings in schemes that proved to be worthless. People have lost their homes due to flood and fire.

Carter M. Comaford, who heads an executive placement firm in New York and Los Angeles, also conducts a training program for executives who are looking for new positions. Many of the men and women who take part in that program are in a state of shock when they begin. These people, most of them in higher income brackets, considered themselves at least as immune to unemployment as we did to our predicament, and their emotional upheaval can easily be compared to ours.

Like us, these business executives have had to face their emotions head on. What was surprising to Mr. Comaford at the beginning of his program was the regularity with which his clients reported improvement in other areas of their lives: family stability and community participation. Like us, after their initial shock, they learned to take the bull by the horns. These people emerged from their experience strengthened and enriched in areas of their lives of which they were previously unaware. They were able to make more meaningful contributions not only to their subsequent executive positions but to their families, friends, and neighbors as well.

It would be very difficult to tell any woman contemplating a mastectomy that it could have any positive results in her life. It would be even more difficult to tell her that she could develop more womanliness and even femininity than she ever thought possible. How could anyone, hobbling around in the confines of the bandages ever believe that she could one day move more gracefully than ever before? How could any woman facing the scar for the first time be expected to foresee the day when, stepping out of the shower to face a full-length mirror, she would see the reflection of a firmer, healthier body? How could she be told that her relationships with men could develop a new dimension and become more meaningful than ever?

Like the legendary phoenix that is supposed to be reborn from its own ashes, from the ashes of despair, despondency, anger, and grief following a mastectomy, a woman can be reborn into a new awareness of life. A body that was formerly considered a burden can become a source of joy. Free time, once considered something that had to be "killed," can turn into luxurious solitude and a chance to replenish one's inner self.

I cannot promise anyone instant anything or miracle marvels. Rome wasn't built in a day and our bodies aren't going to be rebuilt in a day. As a result of my own mastectomy I embarked on an "operation bootstrap" that formed a foundation for a radical improvement in my life. I developed a series of exercises to be done slowly and carefully and became aware of parts of my body that I had never known before except as abstract words from anatomy books. As a result of this unfolding body awareness, I changed my eating habits completely—no small feat for a gourmet cook as well as a gourmet eater!

If there was any magic ingredient involved, it was determination and the awareness that it *could* be done. The only miracle I can offer is the realization that there are no miracles, unless the process of growth and development itself can be called a miracle.

Fair warning: When you decide to take the bull by the horns, the road ahead can be a rocky one. There's nothing like a major illness to bring out the noble altruism in people, usually at the expense of the person who has undergone that illness. Sometimes, we can present less of a threat to others in a weakened condition than we can in a strengthened one. Well-meant advice such as "Take it easy—you've been through so much" and "Get a complete rest—you mustn't exert yourself" could lead to feelings of dependency, loss of self-esteem, slackened body tone, and, worst of all, a frozen shoulder—loss of mobility in the shoulder area, which, in turn, leads to limited movement of the entire arm.

The clenched fist anti-mastectomy segment of the women's Anti-mastectomy sentiment runs high in emotional aftereffects of a mastectomy as well. Stories about women breaking down completely following a mastectomy, to the point of not being able to function physically, mentally, or emotionally, abound. No mention is ever made of the ability to cope with life *prior* to surgery in the case of these women. Like all misleading rumors, nothing is said about the number of women whose mastectomies became springboards to greater self-fulfillment.

As with any devastating experience—accident, divorce, loss of a loved one, or drastic change in life-style—a woman is at a crossroad after a mastectomy. One path leads to inaction, indolence, languor, and self-pity. The other leads to action, self-awareness, and self-fulfillment. We cannot remain at a standstill because life does not remain at a standstill. Having been diagnosed with breast cancer, we chose competent medical care. Following a mastectomy, a woman has a choice in her total life adjustment—indolent self-deterioration or new growth and determination.

Because you are reading this book, there is no question as to which path you will choose.

11
Diet

There may be a tendency to gain weight following a mastectomy. In many instances, overeating is a reaction to emotional stress. Some women regard the immediate post-hospital period as one of continuing convalescence. Thus, the physical inactivity and resulting boredom can become a major cause of overeating. Hovering friends and relatives usually decide that a woman has to eat to regain her strength. Some women feel that a weight gain is indicative of a guarantee that they are in perfect health. Others feel that displaying a hearty appetite and the ability to enjoy food serves as a message to the world that recovery is complete.

Whether or not you've ever had a weight problem, you may have to seriously reassess your eating habits following a mastectomy. For a variety of reasons, general health will have to be considered seriously, and body image, which has received a severe blow as a result of surgery, will have to be maintained or improved. For those who've regarded eating as a reward, the satisfaction will shift from immediate, momentary gratification to long-range improved body awareness and appearance. In conjunction with a well-planned exercise and physical activity program, a balanced diet in itself can become a reward. Rich sauces, gravies, and fancy desserts lose their temptation when a feeling of general well-being takes over.

Too much has been said and written about balanced diet to bear repitition here. The same applies for foods to be avoided. Everyone knows that an apple for dessert is more beneficial than apple pie a la mode. But not everyone knows that increased body awareness makes the apple more appealing. A taste can be cultivated for the simpler foods in their natural forms just as a taste was once cultivated for elaborate, decorative nutritionally bankrupt foods. The United States has been called the most overfed and undernourished country in the world. The American diet has been accused of being the culprit for medical disorders ranging from acne to heart disease. Our food industry places more emphasis on packaging and advertising of food products than it does on nutritional content. We overstuff our guests as a gesture of hospitality as we gorge ourselves as a gesture of politeness when we are the guests. We are being increasingly alerted to the dangers of increased use of chemical additives in food products. In addition, reports of lowered sanitation standards in processing of meats and packaged food products border on the scandalous as well as the stomach-turning.

The tendency to gain weight following a mastectomy has been noticed in a great many women. Various explanations have been given for this, the most frequent one being that food will be used as a "reward" in times of emotional upheaval. However, many women feel that, following a mastectomy, they have to prove to themselves and others that they are completely cured—the "weight loss as a sign of cancer" myth doesn't die easily.

Following a mastectomy, many women are advised by their doctors to cut down considerably on salt intake and avoid delicatessen-type foods. Since so many people regard food as a source of emotional rather than nutritional satisfaction, they can only consider a shift in diet away from the "yum-yum" category to nutritionally sound foods as the height of punishment and deprivation. This does not have to be the case. Discovery of whole grains, fruits, and vegetables, either raw or lightly steamed, can be as enlightening as our earlier discoveries of marshmallow fudge sundaes, Sacher torte, or galantine of chicken in heavy cream sauce. One of the rewards of cultivating the habit of eating simpler foods is the absence of that leaden feeling that overtakes us after having eaten heavy, highly indigestible food.

Before you make any decisions concerning your future diet, however, you will want to discuss the following subjects with your physician:

- What foods, if any, are to be avoided?
- What foods, if any, should be emphasized?
- Any restrictions on drinking?
- Advisability of going on any particular diet, whether through a diet club or a diet published in a book or magazine.
- Advisability of taking vitamins other than those that may have been prescribed for you.

WEIGHT REDUCTION

Whether or not you have had a weight problem before the surgery, a few words of caution will have to be said about fad diets, instant reducing plans, and diet pills. The essential word is *out*. They are risky for anyone, but for us, it means asking for trouble. Besides being ineffective and nutritionally unsound, fad diets are often dangerous. The side effects of reducing pills, often containing barbiturates or stimulants, are being brought to the attention of the public. It usually takes two or three months after publication of a best-selling "miracle" diet book for the lawsuits to start pouring in. The authors have usually "forgotten" to mention side effects such as dizziness, heart attacks, and possible genetic damage to unborn children. No lawsuits are brought for failure to achieve the promised weight loss or to maintain any weight loss that may have come about. The readers of such books merely wait for the next miracle diet to come along.

Special diets and "diet reducing plans," usually in conjunction with some overpriced and undereffective exercise gadget, are constantly being advertised, especially in women's magazines, appealing to every age range from teen-ager to matron. Many of these include pills, some of which have been found to contain hormones. Not only have these proven worthless in achieving weight loss, but any pill containing hormones must receive special scrutiny for the general public—and especially so for us. It can take from several months to several years before government health and consumer fraud agencies catch up with the promoters of these products, and in many cases it has taken several million dollars out of consumers' pockets as well. For some reason I've never been able to discover, the magazines that advertise these products are always held blameless. The manufacturing companies usually react by declaring bankruptcy and incorporating under another name before promoting their next miracle—usually the same basic components as the previous miracle, with the trade name changed.

In recent years there has been a proliferation of weight-loss groups or clubs. For an initial registration fee and a nominal weekly fee thereafter, members are given a diet to follow and are required to attend weekly meetings to report their progress. Group therapy tactics, from public weighing in to group ostracization for "culprits" (those who have gained weight since the previous meeting) are used. These clubs point with pride to the graduates who have lost considerable amounts of weight—100 pounds or more. They are a little less vociferous about the reportedly high percentage of former members who have regained the weight (and then some) after having completed the program. I, personally, cannot endorse fear of public humiliation or other shaming techniques as effective motivation to lose weight or improve any other aspect of body image. Self-respect can only tend to be negated by any form of taunting or mockery.

Besides the often short-lived effects of group dependency as a weight-loss technique, post-mastectomy women have a more important reason to scrutinize the techniques of any reducing club—a reason that should receive serious consideration by non-mastectomy women as well. Although many of these groups base their diets on sound nutritional planning, they also rely quite heavily on chemical substitutes and artificial flavorings—especially sweeteners—and encourage increased use of spices and seasonings.

Weight Watchers, the original weight-reducing club, developed its diet in conjunction with qualified nutritionists of the U.S. Department of Health. In many ways, the diet is nutritionally balanced, and members of Weight Watchers are eating balanced diets, often for the first time in their lives. However, the emphasis placed on chemicals and the encouragement for the use of artificial sweeteners and flavorings makes this program literally hazardous for anyone with a history of cancer. Although there had been murmurings about the relation of diet to various forms of cancer for years, it was only in December 1975 that funds were allocated by the government to research this aspect more thoroughly.

Preliminary findings point to a diet high in animal fats and chemicals as a possible culprit in breast cancer, as well as being a possible culprit in other forms of illness totally unrelated to cancer. There is certain handwriting on the wall, which no post-mastectomy woman can afford to ignore.

What should be considered most carefully by any prospective member of a weight-losing group is their reliance on an intake of "empty" foods (foods lacking in caloric value) rather than trying to attack the underlying emotional problem and ingrained habits of regarding gratification in the form of food as a substitute for fulfillment in other areas of life—interpersonal relationships, creative self-expression, and the enjoyment of a fully active body. Unquestionably, every weight-reducing club has its own psychological techniques, in addition to its own diet. Although some of them undoubtedly place emphasis on living an emotionally fulfilled life, thereby attacking the root of destructive eating habits, others do use shame by public humiliation as its strongest incentive for its members to lose weight. How many people who have had their feelings of inadequacy reinforced by this technique can only be guessed at. If you're considering joining a weight-reducing club, you might want to check into some of their methods of keeping their members in line, along with the diet. Although some of these clubs require a doctor's approval before accepting a new member, many of them simply don't bother. If you are considering joining one of these groups, make sure you have a copy of their instructions and diet-related literature to discuss with your doctor. *Any* diet you plan to start should receive your doctor's approval beforehand, anyway.

SHOPPING FOR NUTRITION

Although we all tend to equate diet with weight, body tone, and figure beauty, many of us tend to forget that it is also the firmest foundation for all-around beauty care—skin, nails, hair, and that indefinable "healthy glow."

A change in eating habits will have to be accompanied by a change in food-shopping habits. The supermarket may have to give up its supremacy in favor of fruit and vegetable stores, meat and fish markets and, to a degree, health food stores, which will be discussed more fully later in this chapter. As you become nutrition-aware, you will learn to read labels more carefully. It is especially in the area of the snack foods and prepared and convenience mixes that a little more of your time is required. Careful study of the listing of ingredients on a bottle of commercial salad dressing can become an incentive for anyone to consider the merits of an oil-and-vinegar dressing prepared at home. As some of the printing on labels becomes almost microscopic when the manufacturer lists the ingredients, a small, pocket magnifying glass can come in handy as a regular feature of your food shopping expeditions.

Much attention has been given lately to the subject of health foods and organic foods. While minimizing the intake of additives and chemicals can only benefit anyone's diet and, consequently, general health, we cannot simply lump all food stores into two categories, with the health food stores being the good guys and the supermarkets being the bad guys.

Basic foods, such as rice, nuts, cheese (rather than "cheese products"), eggs, honey, milk, and dried fruits, are available at supermarkets at considerably lower prices than at health food stores. The so-called health foods, such as wheat germ, honey, and yogurt, are also readily available in supermarkets. Some basic food products that are comparatively free of additives are available in health food stores, which I rely on for oils, peanut butter, and salt-free seasonings. However, where the prepared food products are concerned, such as canned foods, baking products, and "diet supplements," the same magnifying glass you use in the super-market is called for. This will reveal at least the same proportion of additives as many of the food products to be found in super-markets. A close look at the labels of the canned meat substitutes, usually soybean derivatives, reveal them to contain at least as many chemicals as a supermarket canned meat product. A closer look at the labels of so-called natural margarines often indicates the presence of artificial food coloring and other ingredients to prevent spoilage.

If your doctor advised you to eliminate or cut down on salt, it would be wiser not to grab for the nearest package of salt substitute so prominently on display in health food stores. The labels of these often contain warnings such as "Do not use except under the advice of a physician." I have found a seasoning called, Veg-It, a blend of dried herbs, vegetables, and yeast, to be a very satisfactory replacement for salt, of which I was a former near-addict.

Another trap to be avoided in health food stores is the use of the word *organic*. While some organically grown foods are unquestionably tastier and more nutritious than those grown in chemically treated soil, their spoilage rate is higher. Also, it has been reported that quite a few health food stores have relied on nearby supermarkets when their own supplies of "organic" fruits and vegetables have run out. Reports of cockroaches and other vermin (undoubtedly organic) would also make it prudent to choose the prepackaged food basics, no matter how homey the burlap bags of rice, millet, soybeans, and other grains appear.

While health food stores can undoubtedly be beneficial in offering a larger selection of additive-free basic foods, there are aspects of these stores that are highly questionable and should be regarded suspiciously by any responsible, aware consumer. The vast assortments of "diet supplements," vitamin compounds, and purported weight-loss and weight-gain preparations are regarded as suspect by qualified practitioners in every area of health care. It is, unfortunately, the health food stores that provide the major outlet for food faddists, unqualified nutritionists, self-styled doctors, and purveyors of pills and books offering miracle cures to promote their products and theories. As in the case of any product promoted by unqualified self-styled "experts," many of them are, at best, worthless and at worst, misleading and dangerous. Chapter 20 discusses fully the tactics of quacks, charlatans, and misguided zealots.

Among the seemingly harmless preventatives and/or cures promoted at health food stores are vitamins and vitamin-based preparations. The megavitamin controversy* will rage for a while. In the meantime, it has been proven that vitamins A and D can be toxic in overdoses. While nonprescription vitamins are probably relatively harmless in limited quantities, reaching for a bottle of vitamin pillls instead of planning a nutritionally balanced diet is the equivalent of trying to repair a crumbling building with a coat of paint. Your doctor may have prescribed vitamins for you. If you plan on taking any others, check with your doctor first. Fads occur

---

*The megavitamin theory is that unusually high doses of vitamins can be used to prevent or cure specific illnesses, from the common cold to schizophrenia.

in "miracle vitamins" at least as regularly as they do in "miracle diets."

As vitamin C had earned itself a reputation as the battler of the common cold, so did vitamin E earn itself a reputation as the "sex vitamin." Unfortunately, the common cold and impotence still exist.

Another danger of health food stores is their willingness to promote and sell products under the general heading of vitamins, which, on further examination, turn out to be harmful drugs. Recently, the most glaring example of this practice was the scandal involving B-17, or laetrile, which was discovered to cause cyanide poisoning.

The subject of diet cannot come up without raising the question of drinking, which many people consider to be part of diet. When I embarked on my own diet/exercise program, I found that my customary glass (or two) of wine with dinner, although offering a temporary illusion of relaxation and mellowness, actually became a deterrent to the genuine relaxation I was beginning to experience as a result of improved body tone. If your doctor gives you the go-ahead, and you can limit your liquor intake to moderate social drinking, fine. However, there have been cases involving women who were light or moderate drinkers prior to a mastectomy developing an increasing dependency on alcohol following the mastectomy. If any woman finds herself developing this tendency, or a growing reliance on tranquilizers or sedatives, she should look into the question of seeking psychological help immediately.

For those who regarded eating as a prime source of satisfaction, it can seem like insult added to injury to undergo a complete change of eating habits after a mastectomy. But, as body awareness increases, dependency on food as a source of consolation or comfort decreases, and when results of proper diet become apparent in improved appearance and mental outlook, the foods that were formerly rejected because they were "good for you" change their status from punishment to reward.

12
All-Around Beauty Care

Following a mastectomy, the question of appearance as a basic component of femininity takes on an added dimension. Some women suffer feelings of despondency and futility and adopt a "What's the use?" attitude. Others overcompensate and make an obsession out of surface appearance, regarding the mastectomy as evidence of loss of womanhood, loss of youth, or tragically, both. These women tend to assume the desperate, haunted appearance of the legendary fading movie queen. Either extreme is self-destructive, whether or not a woman has undergone a mastectomy. Anxieties are only compounded by advice from well-meaning outsiders, such as "You mustn't worry about your looks" or "Go out and spend the day at a beauty parlor—it will give you a lift."

Many women have found that their looks have improved following a mastectomy for a variety of reasons. A heightened self-awareness invariably includes an appearance awareness. One of the benefits of having fully faced the loss of a part of one's own body is the realization that we are entitled to pay more attention to that which remains without becoming defensive about being vain. A woman is not called vain if she wants to maintain a beautiful garden to bring enjoyment to everyone who sees it. Why should she be called vain if she wants to create beauty in herself for the same reason?

As in the case of the non-mastectomy woman, a balance of proper nutrition, sufficient rest and relaxation, sensible exercise, and inner serenity forms the foundations of beauty. Cosmetics and hair preparations can be effective only when they are regarded as secondary to the wellspring of inner beauty. While diet and exercise have long been regarded as the basis of figure beauty, we still have a tendency to think of the head as being completely dissociated from the body where beauty care is concerned. The prevalent thought seems to be: cosmetics and hair preparations from the neck up; diet and exercise from the neck down. But proper nutrition and exercise are as basic to skin and hair vitality as they are to body tone. The fresh fruits and vegetables in your diet will become apparent in your face as well as your figure.

COSMETICS

Your awareness of your appearance is important to you at this time. For many women, the surgery and hospitalization created a financial strain in addition to the physical and emotional problems surrounding the mastectomy itself. This does not mean that you cannot create little luxuries for yourself on a limited budget. These luxuries do not depend on a large financial outlay as much as they do on your own realization that the time and care you devote to yourself can contribute more to your feeling of well-being than the price tag on a jar of face cream.

While this is a wonderful time for you to be creative about yourself, there are precautions to be considered which can be revealed through discussions of the following subjects with your doctor.

- Shaving underarm on affected side
- Use of deodorant on affected side
- Possibility of hair loss if chemotherapy is involved
- Advisability of beauty treatments other than routine beauty salon facial

This could be an ideal time to experiment with makeup. Throwing caution to the winds at the five and ten could provide an opportunity to try eye makeup, colorings, and shadings that we never had the time (or nerve) to sample before. When we're able to take a bath or shower again, we can take a few extra moments to make it a beauty treatment with a body lotion or cream. Lying in a darkened room with your feet raised higher than your head, your face covered with cream or lotion, and your favorite music on the record player with the volume turned low will do more to relax you than a frenzied trip to a beauty parlor where you will be worried about the bill.

Except for face creams and lotions containing hormones, there are no more restrictions on cosmetics for us than there are for the non-mastectomy woman. Of course, *everyone* should exercise particular caution with hair preparations involving chemicals: coloring products, straighteners, and home permanents. Aerosol spray products, such as deodorants and hair spray, are best avoided, as it is impossible to use them without inhaling the superfine mist. Hair-setting lotion is available in pump-type dispenser bottles as well as aerosol cans. As long as we're avoiding aerosol spray products, we might just as well extend them into household cleaning products, where inhalation dangers may be even greater.

If you manicure your own nails, you have to observe the same caution you tell your beauty salon manicurist to do—leave the cuticle alone on the affected arm. Because of the need to avoid cuts and scratches on the affected arm and hand, the post-mastectomy, as well as general beauty precaution that every woman is advised to follow (but few of us ever do) is to use rubber gloves during household cleaning. An electric razor is safest for the underarm area. Ask your doctor about using a deodorant on the operative side.

Some women require chemotherapy as a follow-up to their mastectomy. Some of the drugs used can bring about a temporary hair loss or thinning. Sometimes, women become disturbed by this and go to extreme measures, such as not washing or combing their hair for fear it will fall out. In many instances, this loss is temporary but is, understandably, upsetting. If you feel there is a possibility that you may undergo a hair loss, you might want to get a wig to tide you through this period. If you are aware beforehand that hair thinning is a possibility, you have plenty of time to try the wig styles that you feel are most becoming to you. Your doctor can advise you if any hair loss is to be expected.

Fresh air and outdoor activity are probably more meaningful in the way of beauty treatment than long hours spent in beauty salons. Weather permitting, take advantage of all the fresh air you can get, but as we have to avoid sunburn,* make sure that your affected arm is adequately protected. (See chapter 14, "Clothes.")

COSMETIC SURGERY

Many women, perhaps for the first time in their lives, will give consideration to cosmetic surgery following a mastectomy. For those to whom it would not present a financial problem or those who feel it would be worth the cost, I present the following information about cosmetic surgery. For my medical facts, I spoke to Dr. Randolph H. Guthrie, Jr., chief of Plastic Surgery Services in New York City's Memorial Hospital. This information applies to any woman considering plastic surgery on any part of her body.

Cosmetic surgery is no more of a medical risk for a woman who has had a mastectomy than it is for anyone else. But, as in the case of the breast surgeon himself, the qualifications for plastic surgery are of prime importance.

Cosmetic surgery is a lucrative specialty. Anyone with the letters *M.D.* after his or her name is legally qualified to practice it. As a result, many doctors who have specialized in other branches of medicine have begun to call themselves plastic surgeons. As with every other medical specialty, qualification to practice plastic surgery requires a specialized training residency over and above basic medical training. To be fully qualified as a plastic surgeon, a doctor would have to be a diplomate of the American Board of Plastic Surgery, or, more informally, a board-certified plastic surgeon. Most people are reluctant to ask a doctor what his qualifications are. Even for the less intimidated, asking a doctor if he were board-certified could evoke an evasive response of "I do plastic surgery." A safe precaution would be to call your County Medical Society first and ask, "Is Dr. X a diplomate of the

*The American Cancer Society has an educational campaign aimed at making the public aware of the relationship of overexposure to sunlight to skin cancer.

Illinois Benedictine College
Theodore Lownik Library
Lisle, Illinois

American Board of Plastic Surgery?" Also, your public library will have a *Directory of Medical Specialists* (two volumes), which can be found in the reference section. This directory contains qualifications are. Even for the less intimidated, asking a doctor if he were board-certified could evoke an evasive response of "I do as a result, recently qualified doctors may not be listed.

There is a vast gray area in the field of beauty treatment that does not quite fall into the category of plastic surgery yet goes beyond what we generally regard as a facial, available in most beauty salons. These could include everything from having cold cream slathered on your face and wiped off, to vacuuming, peeling, dermabrasion, and a face lift without surgery. Many of these are relatively harmless. In some cases, they may be decidedly questionable. Even in the relatively harmless methods of treatment, complications could arise, such as burning or cutting, in which instance the beauty expert is neither licensed, qualified, nor equipped to correct the oversight. If you're considering one of these more sensational forms of facial treatment, better check with your doctor beforehand. This could be tantamount to the proverbial ounce of prevention.

It should be pointed out that if a woman regards cosmetic surgery, especially of the face-lift variety, as any kind of panacea for more deeply rooted problems related to "loss of youth," she runs the risk of aggravating already existing emotional problems and, further, she has no money-back guarantee if she is not satisfied with the results. She has no "face-back guarantee," either.

SILICONE BREAST IMPLANTS

When the question of plastic surgery arises in regard to a post-mastectomy woman, most of the emphasis is placed on silicone breast implants as being the main cosmetic priority. Much has been said about the "mutilation" aspects of mastectomies, and these overzealous but misinformed people erringly blame the cosmetic aspect as being the chief cause of psychological aftereffects of a mastectomy. As in many other aspects of mastectomies, while the militant groups have been vociferously denouncing the neglect of the mastectomy woman's needs by the medical profession, the medical profession has been quietly making progress in this area. As a matter of fact, it is probably in the area of reconstructive surgery that innovations are becoming more widespread, as the pioneers in this specialty are making their discoveries known to the entire profession.

It was for this reason that I went back to Dr. Guthrie, himself one of the pioneers in improving the implant process to the point where its medical risk would be made absolutely minimal. While, at this writing, comparatively few such operations have been performed, enough information is available so that every post-mastectomy woman can weigh the pros and cons of the process and decide if she wants to seek further consultation about the feasibility of an implant in her particular case.

According to Dr. Guthrie, the procedure can be performed on a large number of mastectomy women. There are two particular instances where complications would arise: when skin grafting has been done as part of the original mastectomy; and if *extensive* radiation therapy has taken place. These two factors do not rule out the possibility of surgical implant, but additional procedures would have to be integrated with the surgery.

When the implant is performed by a fully qualified plastic surgeon experienced in this procedure, there is usually no problem to the patient in future cancer detection methods as a result of the implant, for although it is opaque or semi-opaque to X rays, the breast tissue around it can be seen, so that a mammography is valuable.

In most cases, two operations, three months apart, are required to complete the procedure. The first is the insertion of the implant itself (also referred to as an internal prosthesis); the second involves the application of the nipple, usually a skin-grafting procedure. The total surgical cost may be about the same as that of the mastectomy itself, but accompanying hospitalization costs would be reduced considerably, as each operation requires only two days of hospitalization. Although health insurance plans usually cover hospitalization costs, the procedure would probably come under the heading of cosmetic surgery, and it would be a good idea to check your coverage beforehand.

The implant procedure itself restores the mound of the breast and the nipple only. Any work in the surrounding area, such as filling in depressions under the collar bone or under the arm, would require additional work, such as grafting from other parts of the body. As virtually every mastectomy is different, so would virtually every plastic surgery case have its specific requirements and, understandably, the extent of work done during the mastectomy itself will, to a large degree, determine the feasibility and practicality of reconstruction work. Although the same surgeon who performed the mastectomy will probably not be performing the implant (unless the implant was done at the time of the mastectomy), it is the surgeon who should be consulted first as to the advisability of follow-up reconstructive surgery.

Dr. Guthrie is quick to point out that a "perfect match" is not likely to result. Cleavage will be restored so that the woman can wear low-cut bathing suits or evening gowns, but if a woman hoped to restore her preoperative appearance exactly or did not want "any reminder of the experience," she would be well-advised to give serious consideration to just what she hoped the implant procedure would accomplish. There have undoubtedly been instances where a woman has had cosmetic surgery to reduce the size of the existing breast to match the implant more closely, but this is a highly risky procedure for a woman with a history of breast cancer. The scar tissue formed on the remaining breast could seriously interfere with detection procedures and, as we all know, the remaining breast will have to be examined regularly.

Dr. Guthrie also points out that the implant procedure restores appearance but not function. In other words, it would not interfere with any physical activity in the chest or arm area, but neither would it correct any problem, such as removal of the chest muscles or lymph nodes, which occurred as a result of the mastectomy itself.

Of course, a prosthesis would not have to be worn when an implant is performed. Nor would the weight and balance questions have to be considered, as the implant would restore any weight that was lost as a result of the mastectomy.

If you have discussed the feasibility of an implant with your breast surgeon and would like to consult further with a plastic surgeon, you could get a recommendation from the Plastic Surgery Service, Memorial Hospital, 444 East 68th Street, New York, New York 10021. Also, your local County Medical Society could give you information in locating a qualified specialist in this area.

(If you do wind up considering a silicone implant after a mastectomy, discuss the following questions with the plastic surgeon:

• Will the procedure be "simple," i.e., will additional work have to be done in the surrounding area?
• If radiation was involved, what additional procedures may be necessary, or what complications may develop?

I cannot close a chapter on beauty without a word about inner beauty, the fountain from which it all flows. Certainly, we've been through an inner turmoil as a result of the mastectomy. All the more reason why serenity and inner peace and learning to appreciate the joys and beauty of life around us—qualities that should be developed by every woman—should be developed by us.

13
Exercise

To many people, the word *exercise* means, at best, punishment; at worst, extreme punishment. Exercise does not have to be a chore. The exercises in this chapter are designed for slow motion and grace. There is no "push a little harder" or "bend a little farther." These exercises are designed to meet the needs of your body, not vice versa. The arm exercises following surgery must be done to regain full motion of the arm. The exercises here are meant to stimulate total body awareness and to make us realize, once again or for the first time, that our bodies are an expression of the harmony within us.

Along with these exercises, you might want to look into whatever post-mastectomy exercise programs your community may have to offer. This, in addition to the exercises presented here, should be undertaken *only with your doctor's approval.* As time goes on, you may feel ready to join an existing exercise or dance class that encourages you to proceed at your own pace.

EXERCISE PROGRAMS

As Terese Lasser developed the post-mastectomy arm exercises that are in use in so many hospitals today, so has another foresighted post-mastectomy woman, Helen Glines Kohut, developed a community post-mastectomy program including exercise. At this writing, Ms. Kohut's program, ENCORE has been pilot tested in thirty YWCAs throughout the country. ENCORE, incidentally, is an acronym for the purpose of the program: Encouragement, Normalcy, Counseling, Opportunity, Reaching out, Energies revived.

Ms. Kohut is a registered nurse and has had ballet training as well. As a ballet instructor at the Princeton, New Jersey, YWCA, she asked the YW if it would donate the use of its facilities while she, in turn, donated her time for a special class for post-mastectomy women. Ms. Kohut, who had undergone her mastectomy in 1964, was aware of the effort, strain, and often discouragement that accompany the recovery process. The YW offered its cooperation, and the ENCORE program got its start. Today, ENCORE has expanded to include gentle, rhythmic exercises to music, swimming exercises where facilities permit, advice on clothing and prostheses, and rap sessions where post-mastectomy women can trade shop talk in a congenial, friendly atmosphere with other women who they feel will understand their problems. Women of all age groups (including women who had never been in an exercise program before in their lives) have benefited from ENCORE both physically and psychologically.

The prime value of ENCORE, according to Ms. Kohut, is the nonclinical atmosphere of a community facility and the feeling these women have of taking part in full, active lives. It is also encouraging for the woman who had her mastectomy only recently to see other post-mastectomy women in more advanced stages of recovery. ENCORE accepts post-mastectomy patients as early as three weeks after surgery, with their doctor's approval. The program was first approved by an advisory committee composed of members of the Medical Center of Princeton, and at this writing, ENCORE has undergone a thorough study by a national committee of medical experts, prior to the program's becoming available nationally.

To Ms. Kohut, the most rewarding aspect of ENCORE can best be typified by her statement, "When these woman first come to class they're wrapped in a cocoon of fear and self-doubt. Gradually, they emerge to value themselves as women once again."

Although ENCORE is a YWCA project, the YW is making training programs available to non-profit community programs, as they realize that not every city has a YW. If you are interested in having an ENCORE program started in your community, contact ENCORE, YWCA National Headquarters, 600 Lexington Avenue, New York, New York 10022.

While the ENCORE program is designed for women who have recently gotten out of the hospital, the foresight, enthusiasm, and desire to help is extending to other dance and exercise instructors who are eager to meet the needs of post-mastectomy women after the immediate post-hospital needs have been met. Dorothy Hill, of the Manhattan School of Dance in New York City, has a background in physical therapy as well as ballet, and most of her students are at least one year post-mastectomy. Because of the demand for her program from women in all parts of the country who are unable to attend her classes, Dorothy is now preparing a home exercise program consisting of a cassette tape with music and instructions, as well as an illustrated booklet describing the movements. This cassette/booklet set should retail for about $35, and information on ordering it can be found in Appendix C.

Michaeline Kiss conducts the Yoga for Health School in New York City. Michaeline's background includes having developed special classes for people with varying physical limitations —cardiac disorders, back problems, and blindness. Recently she has begun to integrate post-mastectomy women into her regular yoga classes, as soon as three months following surgery, with doctor approval.

BODY AWARENESS

Exercise and diet go together. Many women have found that as their body awareness increases and becomes a source of fulfillment and joy, the tendency to regard food as a prime source of pleasure decreases proportionately. Improved body toning is invariably accompanied by improved mental outlook. So many women say, "Oh, but I'm not athletic." While exercise may be a preliminary for sports activity, it is not, in itself, a sport. For the woman who has been active in sports and is eager to resume full participation, these exercises are an ideal interim step. For the woman who never considered herself athletic, the exercises by themselves will benefit her in improving body tone and grace—the awakening of the entire body. And as the awareness of the entire body develops, so does the emphasis on the missing breast diminish.

The exercises illustrated in this chapter are based on yoga principles, but they are not standard yoga *asanas* or positions. However, the principle of slow motion applies, and the basic tenet of yoga philosophy, "Never go beyond your capacity," applies to these exercises as well. If you want to exercise at home and go beyond the exercises described here, I would suggest the books of Richard Hittleman. My own favorite is his *Yoga Twenty-eight Day Exercise Plan*. Because the book is so beautiful, not only in its illustrations, but in its philosophy, I will take the liberty of quoting from it here:

> A beautiful woman radiates from within; her complexion glows and her eyes shine. Her movements and gestures are posed and graceful, they flow with a natural rhythm. The entire body of a self-realized woman will be beautiful because she is deeply aware of her inner beauty and this awareness is transferred to all who come in contact with her. The humility, compassion and love of a beautiful woman are genuine and a mystical quality is present in her aura.*

Of course, many of us will never get to the headstand or some of the other advanced positions. But the harmonious flow of movement, so eloquently communicated by Mr. Hittleman's writing, can manifest itself in the simplest gesture. It is this sense of grace and harmony in motion that is more basic to womanhood than the presence of breasts. One of my favorite legends in Greek mythology is that of Artemis, the huntress and moon goddess, having had one breast removed for ease in handling the bow and arrow. The loss of a breast does not mean the loss of grace and rhythmical gestures. On the contrary, the loss of a breast can mean the beginning of total body awareness. But it does take motivation, determination, and regular practice.

---

*Richard Hittleman, *Yoga Twenty-eight Day Exercise Plan* (New York: Workman Publishing Company, 1969) p. 155.

EXERCISE INSTRUCTIONS

In the drawings in this section, the figure is shown in a leotard and tights in order to clearly illustrate details. The figure is also shown as wearing a prosthesis and brassiere, as this provides maximum comfort during physical activity. You will, of course, be wearing clothing that is most appropriate and comfortable for you. While in the hospital you will be wearing a loose, comfortable nightgown. At home, you may be wearing a loose, free-flowing robe or any other kind of clothing that allows freedom of movement. In the beginning, while you are still bandaged, the deep-armhole shirt provides the most comfort. Below this you may wear loose-fitting slacks, preferably made of a knit fabric, or ballet tights or opaque panty hose with the feet cut off at the ankles. Barefoot tights are available at dance specialty stores, but panty hose with the feet cut out are equally effective and considerably less expensive.

Bare feet are essential during these exercises, except when you are in the hospital, when the flat, nonskid slippers should be worn. It is also important that these exercises be done on a hard floor. A thin, nonskid mat may be used to stand on, but not a towel or bath mat, as they have a tendency to slide on the floor. Deep, heavy-pile carpeting should be avoided, as it interferes with the necessary "grip" on the floor.

Remember, these exercises do not *replace* the arm movements prescribed by your doctor. They are in addition to the arm exercises, and should be undertaken *with your doctor's approval only.* As you regain full motion of your arm, you will ease out of the hospital exercises and into normal activity in everyday life. As these exercises become part of your daily routine, you will find that you progress in your reaching and bending without any conscious effort or awareness on your part. Therefore, you will start off only in the beginning stages with the realization that progress will come slowly and naturally, much like the growth of a plant.

These exercises will appear to be no different from countless exercises you have seen illustrated in books and magazines. The difference is in the slow motion and the "holding" at your extreme level, so there are no sudden jerks or pulls to hamper your progress.

These exercises work with body motion, not against it. As you read the instructions, you will see that emphasis is shifted from how far you can bend or stretch to how slowly you get into the position and how slowly you get out of it. These exercises are the extreme opposite of calisthenics, which require rapid, straining motions. The principle here is to move slowly and rhythmically and to stop *just short* of the point of strain. In these exercises you are developing harmony of movement, not punishing your body.

All instructions include a "count"—the first count to get into the position, the second to hold the position, and the third to ease out of the position—no sudden straightening or unbending. In the beginning you will want to observe the count very carefully. As you become accustomed to your own body rhythm, you may prefer to eliminate the count and exercise to music or one of the environmental records described in chapter 19.

It is important that you establish a specific time for your exercises each day, as you do for any responsibility in your day-to-day living. If you have young children, schedule your exercise time for when the children are in school, or if they are of preschool age, when they are asleep. If your friends are in the habit of telephoning frequently, tell them that there is a certain time when you would prefer not to receive phone calls, explaining that your exercise routine is an important aspect of your recovery.

EXERCISE I: SHOULDER ROLL

Starting Position: Stand with feet together, weight distributed evenly on both feet, arms down at sides.

Figure A: Raised Shoulder (see page 94)
To a slow count of 5, raise the operative shoulder as high as it will go comfortably. Do not move any other part of the body.

Hold the shoulder in this position for a count of 2.

To a slow count of 5, lower the shoulder until it is level with the other shoulder.

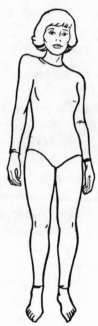

Figure A. Raised shoulder

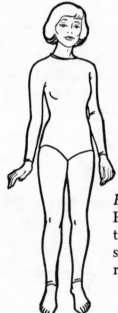

Figure B: Lowered Shoulder
Proceed as with raised shoulder exercise, this time lowering, holding, and returning shoulder to the same counts of 5, 2, and 5, respectively.

Drawings by Bob Smith

Figure C: Forward Shoulder
Proceed as with raised shoulder exercise, this time moving shoulder forward, holding, and returning to the counts of 5, 2, and 5, respectively.

Figure D: Backward Shoulder
This time, move shoulder backward, holding and returning to starting position to the counts of 5, 2, and 5, respectively.

Complete Shoulder Roll
With shoulder raised as in Figure A, form a complete circle with
the shoulder moving backward, for a total count of 6.

Repeat, moving shoulder forward in a complete circle, for a total
count of 6.

Return to starting position.

EXERCISE II: ELBOW RAISE

Starting Position: Stand with feet together, weight distributed
evenly on both feet, arms down at sides.

Slowly raise fingertips to shoulders, keeping elbows close to body.

With fingertips on shoulders, move elbows out to the side to a slow
count of 5.

Raise elbows only until a slight pull is felt on the operative side.

Hold for a count of 2.

Return elbows to sides of body to a slow count of 5.

Note: At first, you may be able to move your elbows only a few inches away from your sides. This is perfectly all right and indicates that you are not forcing, pulling, or straining.

You will eventually be able to raise your elbows to a 45-degree angle from your body (dotted line). Do not attempt to go higher than this 45-degree angle until your doctor gives his approval. After your doctor has given his approval, you will progress in raising your elbows until they are at shoulder level.

Do not attempt to raise your elbows above shoulder level until your doctor gives his approval.

EXERCISE III: TORSO STRETCH

At first glance, this exercise may remind you of kindergarten days, when we all "reached for the ceiling," quickly pulling one arm after the other, feeling the pull in the armpit area only. Because of the slow motion of this exercise, it becomes a torso stretch, with the movement felt in the underarm area from waist to armpit, rather than in the arm itself. In the beginning, you may not be able to raise your operative arm as high as your other one, and it may be more comfortable to keep the elbow of the operative arm slightly bent. It is the slow motion that gives this exercise its effectiveness, *not* how high we reach.

Starting Position: Stand with feet together, weight evenly distributed on both feet, arms raised above head, nonoperative arm straight up, operative arm raised to level of comfort.

Beginning with nonoperative arm, raise arm from shoulder (not fingertips) to a slow count of 5. Stretch should be felt at side of body from waist to armpit.

Hold for a count of 2.

Lower shoulder to count of 5, leaving arm in raised position.

With operative arm at comfortable height, slowly raise from shoulder to count of 5. Do not attempt to straighten elbow or "reach" toward the ceiling.

When the stretch is felt at the side area, hold for count of 2.

Slowly lower shoulder to count of 5, not disturbing the arm position.

Slowly lower both arms down to sides.

EXERCISE IV: WAIST ROLL

Starting Position: Stand with feet comfortable apart, hands on hips.

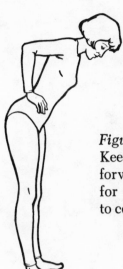

Figure A: Forward Bend
Keeping feet firmly on floor, slowly bend forward from waist to a count of 5. Hold for count of 2; return to starting position to count of 5.

Figure B: Backward Bend
Proceed as in forward bend, this time bending back from waist, to counts of 5, 2, and 5, respectively.

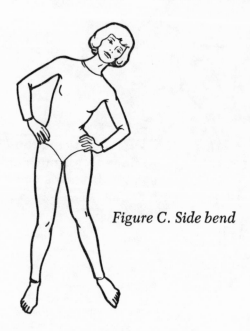

Figure C. Side bend

Figure C: Side Bend
Proceed as in forward bend, this time bending *toward* operative side, holding and returning to counts of 5, 2, and 5, respectively.

Next, bend *away from* operative side, holding and returning to counts of 5, 2, and 5, respectively.

Complete Waist Roll
From starting position, keep feet firmly on floor, *bend from waist only,* forming a complete circle—front, side, back, other side, front. The complete circle should be done to a slow count of 8.

Repeat circle in opposite direction.

Note: In the beginning, you will not be able to bend away from your operative side as easily as toward it. This is natural and to be expected. The important thing is not to strain or force.

Exercise V: Shifting Weight

It is important that this exercise be performed facing a solid, stable piece of furniture, such as a table, desk, bookcase, or dresser. The top should not be much higher than waist level.

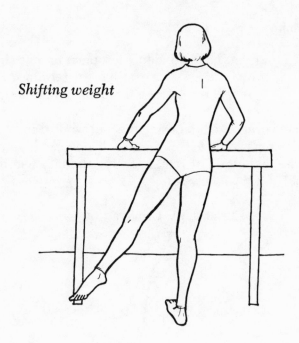

Shifting weight

Starting Position: Facing table, rest hands *lightly* against table-top. Do not grip or lean toward the table.

Start with weight evenly distributed on both feet, keeping knees straight.

Slowly move one foot out to side, keeping both knees straight, to a count of 5. Do not raise foot from floor. Hold for count of 2; slowly return to starting position to count of 5.

Repeat with other foot.

Advanced Position
With hands resting on tabletop, slowly extend foot out to side, this time raising extended foot a few inches off the floor.

Note: If you find when raising the extended leg that you are losing your balance and have to grip the tabletop, you are not ready to raise that foot.

Repeat foot raising, raising other foot.

You may find that you have a balance problem on one side only, often the nonoperative side. When you have determined which is your problem side, repeat the exercise three times on that side.

When you have progressed to raising the foot while standing on the operative side, repeat the exercise on each side, with your hands *away* from the tabletop, but remain facing the table, so that you can catch hold of it if you have to.

EXERCISE VI: LEG STRETCH

Note: This exercise may be done on a mat or rug for comfort.

Starting Position: Lie flat on floor, feet together, arms down at sides.

Keeping knees straight and feet together, slowly raise legs toward ceiling, as illustrated.

With legs up and knees straight, slowly point toes toward ceiling to a count of 3. Hold toes pointed for a count of 2.

Moving ankles only, point toes downward to a slow count of 5, so that heels are toward ceiling. Hold for a count of 2 (dotted line).

Slowly return feet to straight position.

Keeping feet together and knees straight, slowly lower legs to floor.

Note: In the "heels up" position, you will feel a pull in the back of the thighs. These are the hamstring muscles, which may have become tightened due to high-heeled shoes. This exercise, done regularly, will improve balance and posture.

EXERCISE VII: WAIST TWIST

Starting Position: Stand with feet comfortably apart, weight evenly distributed on both feet, hands on hips, elbows pointing outward.

To a slow count of 5, twist from waist only to the left as far as you can comfortably go.

Hold for a count of 2.

Return to starting position to a slow count of 5.

Repeat, twisting from waist to right, holding and returning, to counts of 5, 2, and 5, respectively.

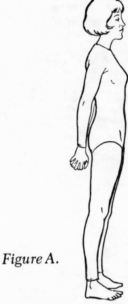

Figure A.

Starting Position: Stand with feet slightly apart, weight evenly distributed on both feet.

Keeping elbows straight, slowly clasp hands as in Figure A. Hold for a count of 5, keeping clasped hands resting against body.

Slowly unclasp hands and return to sides.

Note: If, in the beginning, you cannot clasp your hands behind you, it does not mean there is anything wrong. Merely move your arms back, keeping elbows straight, as though you were going to clasp your hands. Hold your extreme position, whatever it may be, for a count of 2. Eventually, you will be able to clasp your hands behind you.

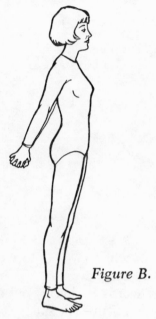

Figure B.

Figure B: Advanced Handclasp
Starting Position: Hands clasped behind you as in Figure A, hands resting against body.

Keeping elbows straight, slowly lift clasped hands away from body to a slow count of 4 (see Figure B). Hold for a count of 2, return clasped hands to body to a count of 4.

Slowly return to starting position.

Note: In the beginning of the Advanced Handclasp, even if you move your hands only an inch or two away from your body, it is a sign of progress. With regular practice, you will be able to raise your clasped hands higher than your waist.

14
Clothes

"What kind of clothes will I be able to wear?" is one of the first questions a post-mastectomy woman asks in relation to practical, everyday living. The words are hardly out of her mouth when she is often answered with a firm "The same clothes you wore before." Period. End of discussion.

In all honesty, however, this answer has to be modified to "*Most* of the same clothes you wore before." As each case is unique, no blanket statement can be made as to what minor variations in style will be advisable for each woman. There are undoubtedly thousands of post-mastectomy women who could wear bikini bathing suits with no one the wiser.

Clothing following a mastectomy can be broken down into two categories—the *immediate* requirements for comfort and ease of dressing; and *long-range* requirements for practicality and fashion. I hasten to add that the immediate clothing needs—wide-sleeved shirts, loose nightgowns, even the so-called temporary breast forms and brassieres—can serve you for years to come.

Because 99 percent of a mastectomy woman's clothing needs can be met in regular department stores, specialty boutiques or "mastectomy departments" have not proliferated as have, for example, maternity departments or shops specializing in maternity clothes. Many corset shops and lingerie departments have made a special effort to stock merchandise specifically for the mastectomy woman, and the specialty shop that carries a line of prostheses and brassieres usually offers a selection of bathing suits and loungewear as well.

However, as necessity is the mother of invention, boutiques catering to the mastectomy woman exclusively have begun to spring up which offer not only clothing but special fitting and alteration services as well. Probably the best known of these are Regenesis and Empire State Mastectomy Salon, both in New York City. Both of these shops plan on opening branches in other large cities, and Regenesis offers a mail-order service for noncustom items. Each of these boutiques was started by a post-mastectomy woman, and they are particularly sensitive to their customers' needs. I would like to take a moment to detail the services offered by each of them.

As women from all over the country come to New York City for surgical care, many of them try to get their clothing needs filled while they are in New York. Once a customer's records are on file at either of these shops, efforts are made so that her future needs can be met by telephone or mail order. As the owners of both these shops are aware of the immediacy and lack of sufficient planning that is inherent in mastectomies, every effort is made to cooperate with close friends and family members so that the patient may have as many of her needs met as possible by the time she is brought down from the recovery room. While the primary service offered is fittings for prostheses and brassieres, every effort is made to offer appropriate hospital and immediate post-hospital clothing. At any given time during business hours, both of these shops are busy waiting on friends and relatives of women who have just had their mastectomies.

The atmosphere at Regenesis is casual and informal and browsing is encouraged. Cathy Smith, one of the owners, reports that many of the women who stop in are prebiopsy and, in some cases, even pre-X ray. These foresighted women want to know what will be available to them should a mastectomy be necessary. Cathy encourages their questions, so that they may be prepared either for themselves or possibly a friend or relative later on. And is there *anyone* who will not, sometime in her life, know of someone who will need these services? Cathy, may your tribe increase—and your boutiques! Write for their catalog (see Appendix C).

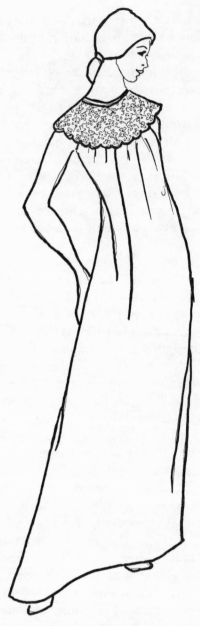

Nightgown with sleep puff by Regenesis, $20

Fashions illustrated by Win Ann Winkler

Hospital gown by Empire State, $20

While most younger women feel that there is definitely a casual, at-home atmosphere at Regenesis, it is at the Empire State Mastectomy Salon that the more mature woman feels most comfortable. Before opening Empire State, Joyce Hart, the owner, had gained the confidence, respect, and frankly, love, of many thousands of women as fitting adviser for the New York City chapter of Reach to Recovery. Being bilateral herself, Joyce is especially well qualified to fit the bilateral woman, as she is aware that, often, each side has different requirements.

For in-hospital needs, both of these boutiques offer nightgowns that serve long-range needs as well. The nightgowns at Regenesis are made of opaque fabrics, featuring high necklines and shoulder coverings. They are soft and feminine in design, and the "sleep puff" is exclusive with Regenesis. This is a fibrefill pad sewn directly into the nightgown. One of their gowns is illustrated on page 108. When purchasing a nightgown for a friend, the customer usually specifies which side will need the puff, as well as the bra and cup size, such as, "Left side, 34-C." Prices for these nightgowns range from $18 to $25, including the puff. However, if puffs are needed on both sides, there is an additional $5 charge.

Empire State offers a nightgown that is suitable for both hospital and at-home wear. Less frilly and feminine than the Regenesis nightgowns, this one serves as loungewear as well. It was designed by Joyce Hart in conjunction with a fashion designer who had a mastectomy, and is illustrated on page 109. Available in opaque cotton, this gown does not require a robe over it. Because of the drawstring neckline, the doctors and nurses can treat the patient by dropping the gown from the neckline, keeping arm movement on the part of the patient to a minimum. Because of its versatility in post-hospital wear, at least one is basic to every post-mastectomy woman's wardrobe. It sells for about $20. Although Empire State does not yet have a complete catalog, an order sheet is available by writing directly to Joyce Hart (see Appendix C).

IMMEDIATE NEEDS

Besides the nightgown, at least one each of temporary breast form and brassiere are needed. Whether or not you choose to wear them in the hospital depends upon your own comfort. If your

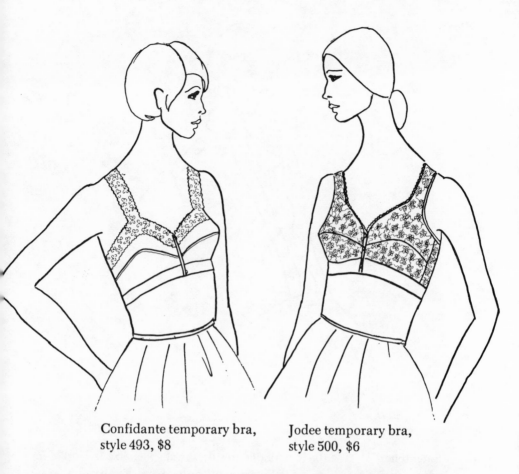

Confidante temporary bra,
style 493, $8

Jodee temporary bra,
style 500, $6

hospital or a Reach to Recovery volunteer provides a form and bra, fine, but you will need an extra set for at home. The bandages may remain on for several weeks, and you will undoubtedly want to launder the bra and pad. Even after you are fully healed, these pads and bras are invaluable as loungewear. The soft forms sell for about $3 and are being made available through department stores and specialty shops. If you have a problem finding them in your area, write to Confidante or Jodee (see Appendix C) for the store nearest you. The "soft bras" or "lounge bras" are illustrated above. The Jodee 500 retails for about $6 and has pockets on each side for the form. Unless a woman is bilateral, she cuts out the pocket on the unaffected side. The Confidante 493 ($8) offers slightly firmer support, and many women prefer to wear it under outer clothing. Both bras have front-hook closings. If the store nearest you doesn't carry either of these two brands, which are designed specifically for post-mastectomy use, you may find

"Ratcatcher" shirt, $10, is available in stores that specialize in clothes for horseback riding. Also available by mail order from Kauffman's, New York, N.Y.

something called a sleep bra, usually made of lightweight stretch fabric. However, make sure it has a front closing, as back closings can present problems immediately following surgery.

The deep-armhole, wide-sleeved shirt will become another basic immediately following surgery. Like the soft bras and forms described above, these, too, will become a mainstay of your long-range wardrobe. You may have some shirts or blouses like these already in your wardrobe. It would be a good idea to have one with you in the hospital to wear home. Often, a shirt suitable for this purpose can be found in active sportswear departments of most stores. The "Ratcatcher," illustrated above, is available at most stores specializing in clothes for horseback riding. Kauffman's, in New York City, is making it available by mail order (see

Wide-sleeved shirt by Regenesis, $30

Appendix C). The one illustrated is available for about $10; another one with tucking down the front is available for about $15. Write and ask them for their Ratcatcher mail order sheet. The shirt illustrated above was designed by Regenesis. Available in navy or white drip-dry polyester, it sells for about $30 and is available through their catalog.

The versatility of these shirts makes them classics. They are handy at the beach, can be worn over turtle-neck shirts, or with an attractive scarf tucked into the neckline.

LONG-RANGE NEEDS

It is when the heavy bandages finally come off that we can make a realistic assessment of the clothes we will be able to wear. This is

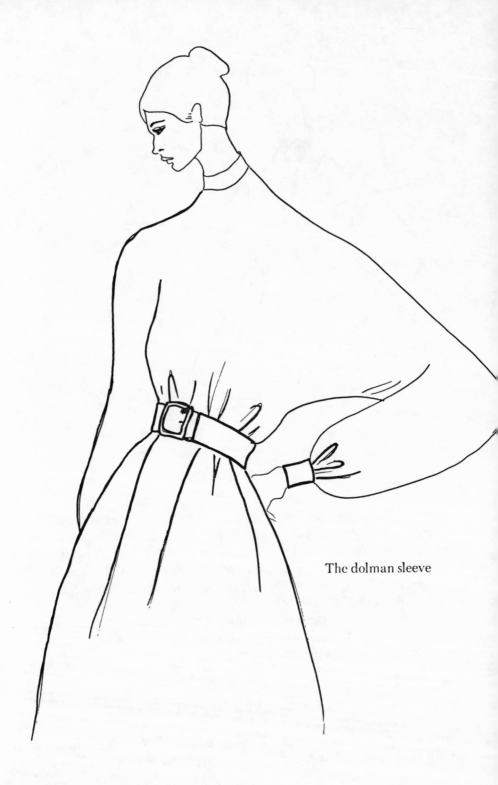

The dolman sleeve

the time when many women say, "I can wear everything I wore before the surgery," and the rest say, "I can wear *almost* everything I wore before the surgery." The "almost" will vary from woman to woman.

If there is one rule that applies to outer clothing for *all* post-mastectomy women, it concerns sleeves. Tight sleeves are not advised because of the tendency toward swelling of the operative arm. This does not mean that *narrow* sleeves are ruled out. It is a matter of fabric and construction of the entire garment, rather than the cut of the sleeve alone. A soft, knit fabric will have the necessary give required, so that there will not be any constriction. Even more important than the width of the sleeve is the cut of the armhole. High-cut armholes can create binding in the underarm and side area. In certain cases, the tendency toward lymphedema may be quite marked, in which case your doctor will recommend a lymphedema sleeve, to be worn under outer clothing. These are available in surgical supply stores. In this case, narrow sleeves are not recommended, and a dolman sleeve, as illustrated on page 114, should be considered for fashion as well as comfort.

The only other general restriction (if you want to call it that) is against tight jewelry on the operative arm. This means no tight bracelets or watch straps, and especially not the upper-arm bracelets or "armlets" that pop up as fashion items from time to time. Granted they may be exotic—but put them on the other arm, please. Remember, the tight jewelry restriction does *not* include loose bangles that can be worn singly or in groups on the wrist. These are quite attractive, especially with long sleeves.

The question of sleeveless dresses and blouses is one that causes quite a bit of concern to women whose incisions extend to the arm. I think all of us, when we first get out of the hospital, become overly preoccupied with the question, "Does anything show?" and can go to extremes worrying whether the prosthesis or temporary form is a fraction of an inch higher than the natural breast. We hope we can put this matter into proper perspective as we regain our "sense of selves" in all areas—physical, mental, and emotional. But if a woman finds herself harping on this subject immediately following surgery, I think she would be wise to stick to looser, less revealing clothing until she is more at ease with the situation. It is *not* the place for well-meaning friends and relatives to say, "Oh, don't be silly—no one will notice, anyway." A woman is not being silly for giving herself the necessary time to ease into a new situation. Adjustment is a series of slow steps, *not* a major, dramatic leap. It is like any growth process; no one would try to make a plant grow by pulling at the stem or forcing the leaves open.

Another area of concern is necklines. Although alterations may be necessary for some low-cut garments, when the alterations are done on the prosthesis and brassiere (see following chapter), most clothes will fit smoothly. Many corsetieres that specialize in post-mastectomy fittings offer alteration services for outer clothing as well.

As far as the overall wardrobe is concerned it is only bathing suits and nightgowns that will require special consideration in future purchases. As I have pointed out before, there are quite a few women who have had simple or modified mastectomies who could easily wear bikinis if they were so inclined. Let's go into each category.

BATHING SUITS

Several manufacturers of prostheses put out a line of bathing suits for post-mastectomy women, most of which have pockets for the prosthesis. They are usually designed with higher necklines and some sort of sleeve or cap sleeve and are sold in lingerie shops that offer postsurgical fittings, as well as lingerie departments of department stores that sell prostheses and accompanying brassieres. The usual price range is $35-$50. They rarely require special alterations. One such suit is illustrated on page 117. A list of manufacturers can be found in Appendix C, and they will send you catalogs as well as the names of the stores nearest you carrying their lines.

Many post-mastectomy women have found attractive bathing suits adaptable to their needs which are manufactured by leading bathing suit companies. These usually have built-in bras and can be altered by a corsetiere to accommodate the prosthesis or soft form (which many women prefer for swimming), or you can sew in a ready-made pocket yourself, following the instructions on page 118. Joyce Hart of the Empire State Mastectomy Salon offers a service where a soft form is sewn into the bathing suit permanently.

Sea Scamp bathing suit, style 703, with matching panty, available for under $40. The suit has a pocket for the prosthesis.

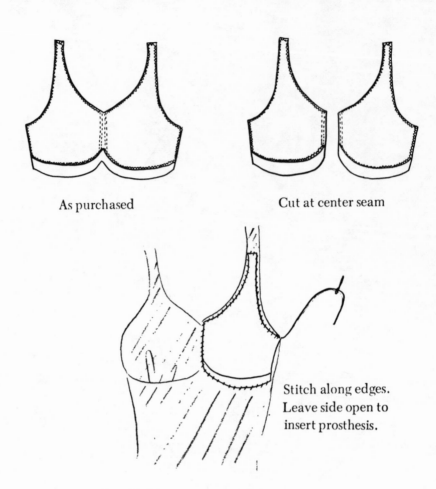

As purchased   Cut at center seam

Stitch along edges.
Leave side open to
insert prosthesis.

Jodee sew-in pockets, $2

These forms are found in regular sportswear or swim departments of department stores, although quite a few corset shops that specialize in postsurgical fittings carry them as well. Prices range from about $25 to $50. Manufacturers whose lines include styles suitable for the post-mastectomy woman include Peter Pan, Sandcastle, Waterclothes, Cole of California, and Rose Marie Reid, among others. Their addresses can be found in Appendix C, and you can write to them for shopping information.

One of my favorite outfits, by Waterclothes, is illustrated on pages 119–120. The bathing suit with black patent leather belt sells for about $35, and the matching skirt is available separately for about $27. Because of its versatility and the fact that it can be worn to a formal occasion as well as the beach, I do not feel that its price is an extravagance.

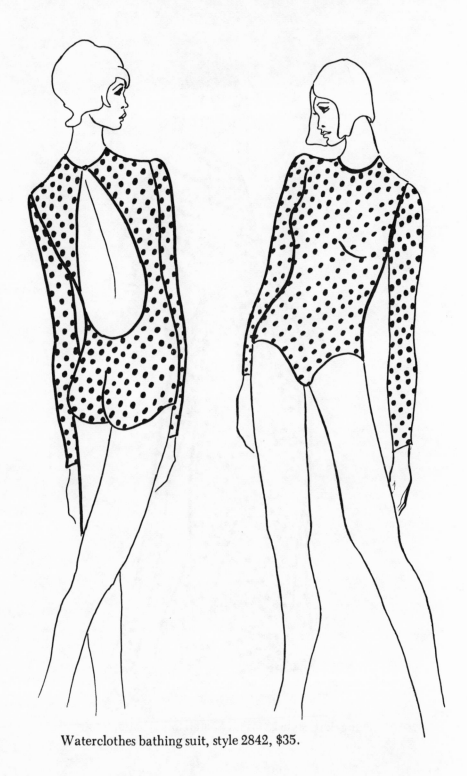

Waterclothes bathing suit, style 2842, $35.

Matching skirt, style 2844, for Waterclothes bathing suit, $27.

Danskin bikini panty and long-sleeved top. Bra and prosthesis can be worn under top.

Because budget is such an important consideration for so many women, I have illustrated several less expensive items that can be used for swimming. I've been swimming in leotards since my pre-mastectomy days, and a bra and prosthesis can be worn under them with no problem. (Better wear underpants, too—especially with the lighter color leotards.) They are available in a variety of sleeve lengths and necklines, and as a quality leotard can be purchased for under $10, I feel they are ideal for the woman who wants to be fashionable on a budget. The outfit illustrated on page 121 is bikini pants and a covered top, both by Danskin. Although they are sold separately, the entire outfit can be purchased for under $15.

Another thing about leotards: They can go anyplace with an appropriate skirt or slacks over them. They are budget wise and especially useful for the woman who takes part in exercise or dance classes, and may be appropriate for those women reluctant to change clothes in a group dressing room or locker room.

Whether you wear a regular prosthesis or soft form with your bathing suit is an individual question. The following chapter explains this decision in choosing the prosthesis.

NIGHTGOWNS

This is the area that can prove to be a painful reminder of the loss, and any woman would be wiser to give in to the inevitable grief she will experience at the beginning rather than attempt to swallow back tears. Fortunately, she will discover that the mastectomy does not relegate her to a life of Mother Hubbard nightgowns. In all fairness, I will have to break down the subject of nightgowns into two categories: sleeping, and intimate moments.

For sleeping, comfort is of prime importance. Whether or not a woman chooses to sleep with a lounge bra and soft pad, or wear a nightgown with a sleep puff, as offered by Regenesis, is an individual decision—as individual as whether or not she wears anything while sleeping.

For the more intimate aspects of nightgowns, the post-mastectomy woman has a selection of soft, feminine nightgowns available to her, as does the non-mastectomy woman. Credit fore-sighted, sensitive designers and manufacturers for taking the

Jodee nightgown with pocket
for prosthesis, $30.

Crepe nightgown or lounge gown by Empire State, $25. It can be worn with the prosthesis if desired.

Regenesis slip, under $15.

Halter-top dress. Pocket can be
sewn in so that the dress can be worn
braless.

responsibility of meeting the needs of the post-mastectomy woman. Regenesis offers a selection of feminine nightgowns, as does the Empire State Mastectomy Salon. Confidante and Jodee, two leading manufacturers of prostheses and bras, are expanding their lines to include nightgowns. One such gown, by Jodee, is illustrated on page 123. This works on the "pocket" principle, and the prosthesis or soft form can be slipped in. If you would like to adapt some of your existing nightgowns to accommodate the prosthesis, the same pocket liners illustrated on page 118 can be used. They are manufactured by Jodee, and sell for about $2 for a set of two.

Many post-mastectomy women prefer no prosthesis or puff with their nightgowns. Styles with high necklines and gathering minimize the lack of symmetry and have a soft, flowing sweep to them which is at least as feminine as some of the more clingy, see-through styles. One such gown, available from Empire State, is illustrated on page 124 and sells for $25. The pockets on the sides are effective in giving the gown a flowing line.

While we're on the question of lingerie, many women feel that sheer blouses and dresses have to be relegated to the "thing-of-the-past" category. Regenesis came up with an answer to that one. The slip illustrated on page 125 sells for about $15, and the built-up lace top and straps cover any scarring or bra straps. Many women find this slip invaluable when trying on clothes in regular department store dressing rooms.

The only other category that may prove limiting for a post-mastectomy woman is evening gowns. Although quite a few women find they can wear low-cut gowns with no problem, others have discovered covered-up elegance—as have so many non-mastectomy women. It is even possible for some women to go braless, as illustrated in the halter-top gown on page 125. Here again, that Jodee pocket form comes to the rescue! This is feasible only when the gown is seamed under the bustline.

In the entire subject of clothes following a mastectomy, the emphasis shifts from "Will anything show?" to "Will my womanhood be set off to best advantage?"

15
The Prosthesis

Anyone could logically ask why I waited until the fifteenth chapter in a book about post-mastectomy adjustment before I got to the subject of prostheses. And I will, just as logically, answer: Because there are too many other immediate priorities in the lives of post-mastectomy women. The theory of the prosthesis being the magic key to every aspect of complete post-mastectomy recovery is one that is going to have to come under closer scrutiny. Granted, the question "Where do I go for a prosthesis?" is often uppermost in the minds of women while they are still in the hospital, but this is because of the hush-hush aura that has surrounded mastectomies for far too long. I would like to applaud the efforts of those manufacturers who openly advertise prostheses and brassieres in newspapers and on radio and television.

Because of all the confusion and conflicting information surrounding prostheses, I would like to shatter a few myths, not only about the right kind of prosthesis (this is like recommending one right shoe size for everyone because it is suitable for some women), but about the role of the prosthesis as consolation prize for a lost breast!

No one knows how many women are walking around with an old stocking or wad of tissue stuffed into their brassieres because they never received adequate information on choosing a prosthesis. Nor does anyone know how many women are using that same stuffed stocking or wad of tissue because the prosthesis with which they were fitted proved to be an uncomfortable, expensive mistake. Prostheses can range in price from $5 to $500, and the higher price tag is no guarantee of suitability in every case. While there are undoubtedly women who feel more comfortable physically and secure emotionally with a prosthesis that "moves" like the natural breast, it is no more their place to prescribe an expensive, silicone-filled form to another woman than it is the place of a woman who is perfectly content with an inexpensive foam form to prescribe it to a woman who may need more weight and balance.

One myth I would like to shatter is that a woman should make her basic prosthesis decision in consultation with a veteran mastectomy woman. While most surgeons will leave the choice up to the patient's preference, *there are definitely instances where certain types of prostheses and brassieres are contraindicated.* After your surgeon has indicated the type suitable for you, it can then be helpful to discuss specific brands and fitters with other post-mastectomy women.

Another myth that has to be shattered is one on the subject of weighting. In many instances, weighting is prescribed as an aid in balance and comfort. But overweighting in a prosthesis can cause as much discomfort for some women as underweighting can create in others. There are many breast surgeons who feel that a weighted prosthesis can become a crutch and that a woman should exercise to restore as much of her balance as possible. The surgeon should be consulted not only as to the advisability of weightedness, but *how much weight,* as well. Most of the heavily weighted prostheses are in the higher price ranges, and many women buy them in the mistaken belief that the higher price is indicative of suitability in their particular case.

The surgeon should also be consulted as to the type of brassiere, as many women are advised to wear wide straps, especially if a heavily weighted prosthesis is indicated. Although a lot of advice is given about altering preoperative brassieres as a viable option to specially designed postsurgical brassieres, your surgeon should definitely be consulted in this matter. If you are considering wearing your preop brassieres, it would be a good idea to take one of them with you during an office visit and show it to your surgeon. Many women are able to wear their previous brassieres after surgery with or without alterations and, besides being economical, it offers the feeling that the change was not so drastic. Ask your surgeon the following questions:

- Is there a specific type or brand name that you require?
- Is there a specific type that is contraindicated in your case?
- Are there any specifications as to brassieres (width of straps, etc.)?
- Is it advisable for you to continue wearing your preoperative brassieres, with or without pockets sewn in? (If you plan on wearing preop brassieres, take one along with you on your next office visit and show it to your doctor.)

Once your surgeon has stated his opinion as to your prosthesis limitations (if any), then *and only then* should you discuss the matter with other post-mastectomy women. These discussions often come up at post-mastectomy discussion groups or rap sessions, and many women gain a feeling of confidence when they can discuss this subject openly.

Comfort and appearance are the prime requisites in a prosthesis. Beyond this, preferences are individual. In some women, fear of being "found out" is strong, and these women prefer features such as "feeling like the natural breast" or a prosthesis that will flatten out when she lies down, as does the natural breast. For others, it becomes a point of pride that they are not fussing over the prosthesis, and if the match is not perfectly symmetrical at all times, they couldn't care less. This is not to imply that any woman will become blasé about a falsie "creeping up under the chin." Every woman wants to be comfortable and make an attractive *overall* appearance, but the frenzied emphasis that has been placed on perfect centering can, in itself, become an obsession.

The fitting itself has become a harrowing experience for too many women, in addition to poorly fitted prostheses and brassieres (not to mention costs). The choice of a fitter is vital. Whenever possible, get a recommendation from your doctor or hospital. A word about the sensitivity on the part of a particular fitter or salon from another post-mastectomy woman could save you a lot of grief, as well.

A few things should be said about the finality of the final prosthesis. If a woman is seriously considering an implant, an expensive prosthesis can be a waste of money, although it must be pointed out that a properly fitted brassiere (essential for *any* woman) and a doctor-approved prosthesis is important during the interim. Even if no implant is considered, there is always the possibility that the remaining breast may enlarge—a fairly common occurrence, and no cause for alarm. Adequate prostheses are available in a moderate price range. The November 1975 issue of *Consumer Reports* covered this subject, and reprints are available from Consumers Union, Reprint Dept., Orangeburg, New York 10962. They are $.40 each.

Joyce Hart, of the Empire State Mastectomy Salon in New York, was of invaluable help to me in preparing the following section. Because so many of her customers had unsatisfactory experiences in previous fittings, she believes that every woman should be armed with information before being fitted and passes these hints on to the reader.

First of all, whenever possible, make an appointment with the salon in advance. This is not a purchase that should be rushed, and at least a half hour should be allowed. Wear close-fitting clothes to see if you want any padding or alterations under the arm or in the shoulder area. The fitter should encourage you to walk around the salon and look at yourself in the mirror from as many angles as possible. Does the prosthesis "move" with you, if that is your basic objective? Lie down, bend forward, lean over, and move your arm as much as possible. How comfortable are you in different positions? If the weighted side feels heavy, don't let the fitter talk you into having to get used to it. Ask if the prosthesis can be exchanged or refunded. Ask about washability of the prosthesis. How long will it take to dry? (Another good reason for always having a spare soft form available.) Many manufacturers claim their prostheses can be used for swimming. Often, it turns out that they can be used for swimming only when wrapped in a plastic bag. Many prostheses are designed with side extensions for women who have undergone full or extended radicals. These can be uncomfortable for the woman who has had a simple or modified radical.

If you are considering a fluid-filled form, consider the possibility of leakage. Because of the thin outer shell, these are especially susceptible to pinpricks or breakage from long fingernails. Usually, a manufacturer will honor a refund should the leak occur at the seam or if the form shows any other indication of faulty construction. But if you do decide on this type, be especially careful when pinning on corsages, jewelry, etc. Also, check with the saleswoman as to the manufacturer's policy on refunds for this reason.

If at all possible, have a brand name or type (foam, air filled, liquid filled, silicone filled) in mind before you go for a fitting—perhaps one recommended by a friend *after* your doctor has approved the type. Ask the fitter to try this type, but also ask for her recommendations about others (assuming your doctor has approved). If a corset shop or department store carries only one brand and it is not what you had in mind, look elsewhere before allowing yourself to be convinced by a sales pitch.

Although most prostheses can be reordered by style number and size from the original place of purchase, initially this is not a purchase that should be made through mail order. Wear your soft form and temporary bra until you can visit a corset salon or department store that offers postsurgical fittings.

If you plan on wearing a prosthesis in a bra that does not have a pocket, pay careful attention to the construction of the prosthesis. Some have foam backing, others have fabric covers. However, some are simply a plastic outer shell with liquid filling and can cause irritation when worn directly against the skin.

Illustrations on pages 132–134 show various brassieres suitable for post-mastectomy needs. Although most prosthesis companies manufacture post-mastectomy bras as well, a standard brand or your previous brassieres may suit your purposes. If you want to sew in a pocket, the same pocket forms described in the previous chapter for bathing suits, nightgowns, and halter dresses can be used (see illustration on page 118).

An exception to this interchangeable prosthesis/brassiere rule is the Jodee form and brassiere. The prosthesis offers an exclusive foldaway shoulder extension, designed to eliminate the need for alterations. The bra, shown on page 134, is designed to ac-

Confidante seamless Moulded Cup, style 480, $18.

Camp Tres Secrete air-inflatable bra, style 024, $15. It is worn without a prosthesis.

commodate this extension. The prosthesis is about $40; prices for brassieres range from $15 to $25.

As important as proper fit is in a brassiere at a time like this, a brassiere should be chosen for feminine flattery as well. Anything that is worn close to you should remind you of your femininity.

Every so often, a post-mastectomy woman hears about an "imitation breast"—usually a liquid-filled form with the outline of a nipple on it, supposedly to be worn under lingerie. These are either pasted directly onto the body or are worn with elastic over the shoulder and are intended to give the illusion that a breast exists where actually one does not. I must admit to an aversion to this sort of device, and if any woman were tempted to wear one, she would

Airway all-Lycra bra, style 3825, $15.

Airway Companion, style 1414, $16.
The long line and wide straps make
it suitable for the fuller figure.

Jodee bra and prosthesis. Cutaway shows shoulder extension feature of prosthesis. Prosthesis about $40; bra about $25.

be very wise to give serious consideration to a surgical implant (see chapter 12). Also, pasting anything onto any surgical scar area is unwise.

Following is a brief description of the basic types of prostheses available. (Shopping information is listed in Appendix C.)

Foam

Available both weighted and unweighted. Unweighted, they have a tendency to move around and ride up. Price range: $5–$20

Air-Filled Plastic

Available as both inflatable forms or form/bra combinations. Can be comfortable during healing period but not recommended long-range. They can overinflate on airplanes, as well as deflate without warning on level ground. Price range: $5–$20 (the higher prices including brassiere).

Liquid Filled

Weighted, available with foam pad backing. Some brands designed to be worn with accompanying brassieres. Usually lighter in weight than silicone filled. Economically sound. Price range: $30–$45.

Silicone Filled

Supposedly the most lifelike; often the most heavily weighted. Unless backed up by foam, can cause discomfort when worn against skin. Some have tendency to expand or lose shape with time. Check claims that they may be worn while swimming. Price range: $90–$130.

Custom Made

They range from foam rubber and liquid-filled forms to exact duplication of the remaining breast by moulded impression. Should be considered carefully, as remaining breast could change size. Price range: $75–$500.

One final word about prostheses and brassiere fittings: Although they are available in surgical supply stores, many manufacturers are incorporating a fashion approach in design, packaging, and selling, and most women prefer to make this purchase in an atmosphere of femininity.

16
Sports and Physical Activity

For the woman who was physically active and participated in sports prior to the mastectomy, the tendency to overcompensate and rush onto the tennis courts or ski slopes can create very real complications and setbacks. For the woman who was physically inactive prior to the mastectomy, the surgery can be used as an excuse never to lift a finger unnecessarily and can contribute to an invalid self-image as well as alienation from her own body. As in any area of living, extremes are to be avoided.

The woman who has never considered herself athletic and never participated in sports would do well by looking into some form of physical activity, even if it is only walking more than she used to. The woman who has been active prior to the mastectomy will have to adopt a policy of moderation and ease back slowly into physical activity. For each woman, the basic exercises described in chapter 13 are essential to her body awareness.

Some people cannot think of the word *sports* without the word *competitive* preceding it. I am using the word *sports* here in relation to body development—not competition. Virtually all medical people involved with mastectomies agree that physical activity is beneficial to the arm area well as the entire body. The woman who is a swimmer has an extra advantage, as this sport is generally regarded as the most complete total body sport. Even for nonswimmers, the ENCORE program (see page 89) has a series of pool exercises designed specifically for arm movement. It's always best to get the go-ahead from your doctor as to when to resume swimming if you've been a swimmer and whether or not it is advisable for you to start if you've been a nonswimmer.

For the recent mastectomy patient, the idea of appearing in a bathing suit can provoke anxiety; reluctance to use public swimming pools, where privacy in dressing rooms is, at best, minimal, can act as a deterrent to something that would benefit the woman. Leaders of YWCA-sponsored swimming programs have taken this factor into consideration, and facilities are made available for the woman who feels she needs complete privacy when changing into a bathing suit.

(If you are accustomed to going to the beach, don't forget about avoiding overexposure to direct sunlight, especially on the affected arm. Chapter 14 illustrates some long-sleeved bathing suits, but whatever kind of bathing suit you wear, take a long-sleeved shirt or sweater with you to put on when you feel you have had enough sun.)

There are as many fully recovered post-mastectomy women on ski slopes, tennis courts, golf courses, and ice-skating rinks as there are in restaurants, department stores, supermarkets, and offices. If you have previously engaged in a particularly strenuous sport such as bowling or tennis, your doctor will advise you when you can begin again. But even when you get the go-ahead, "easy does it" is the byword. If you are a tennis player, a few preliminary sessions simply bouncing the ball with your racquet or hitting the ball against a wall will do a lot for your game—and your arm. If you've been active in sports where balance is essential, such as bicycle riding, skiing, or ice skating, it would be a good idea to practice the balance exercises in chapter 13 before getting on the bike, the ice, or the slopes. Even so, first time out, try to have someone with you.

Many women who have not been physically active prior to the mastectomy (as well as many women who have never had mastectomies) and were having problems of body image become tempted by the plethora of reducing mills and health clubs that offer instant, effort-free spot reducing by means of machinery. Many of these are dangerous as well as unreliable. At best, they could be harmless but costly. They are also suspect from the financial point of view. New York City, in particular, was plagued a few years back by mushrooming health spas and beauty clubs offering bait such as, "Bring a Friend—Two Memberships for the Price of One." Most of these clubs work on a contract basis, and the woman must sign up for a series of visits ranging from months to a year, payment in advance, and money strictly nonrefundable. These clubs declared bankruptcy shortly after their selling campaigns, leaving hundreds of women out thousands of dollars. Another stipulation of many of these clubs is that they require members to sign a release stating they will not hold the club responsible for accident or injury. Serious accidents have occurred as a result of faulty equipment, as well as overcrowded exercise sessions where one woman inadvertantly hit another.

This is not to imply that none of the health clubs offer reliability and safe facilities. However, a post-mastectomy woman considering membership in one of them should determine the club's policy beforehand. Do they require set programs—i.e., do they insist that each member follow a prescribed course of group exercise and use of machinery? Many of the exercise rooms are overcrowded, especially during lunch or after-work hours, and the exercises do not allow for individual needs or possible limitations by specific women. Standards of cleanliness are important in a health club. Check dressing rooms beforehand and see that provisions are made for safekeeping of valuables, such as pocketbooks and jewelry. If you can find a reputable health club that leaves you on your own, such as use of the pool when you want, and use of equipment other than rollers or "spot reducers," it can be beneficial to you.

Some health clubs offer optional massage services. It would be best to check with your doctor before having massages. Although an ordinary Swedish massage is probably perfectly safe, it may be advisable for the masseuse to avoid the affected arm and operative area in your case. Some of the more exotic massage techniques, such as rolfing and acupressure are, at best, questionable, and you should check with your doctor before considering having them.

Saunas and steam rooms are also offered by some health clubs. You should always check with your doctor if you plan on using them. Although they are rarely contraindicated for post-mastectomy patients, there may be other health considerations that would make them inadvisable in your particular case. Total nudity is quite frequent in steam rooms and saunas, but if you are more comfortable in your bathing suit or with a towel around your shoulders, by all means, wear it.

Whether or not you choose to tell the staff of a health club that you've had a mastectomy is up to you. However, if you are urged to lift weights or partake in any strenuous activity and you don't want to mention the mastectomy, you might just say, "My doctor advises against that kind of activity."

Modern dance provides excellent opportunity for full body movement and coordination, exercising the affected arm, and a feeling of rhythm and harmony. Because modern dance is less structured than classical ballet, the student can interpret the movements according to her own needs. Before signing up for a modern dance class, you should discuss your needs with the teacher and find out if she believes in the individual interpretation technique, rather than have everyone doing the same movement at the same time. If you join a beginning adult modern dance class, there will undoubtedly be other women in the class who have their own limitations, such as back problems. An understanding teacher will encourage each student to move according to her own needs.

I am partial to yoga because I feel that it got me moving again after my own mastectomy. Many women who have been in yoga classes prior to a mastectomy are anxious to return as soon as possible and can often do so with their doctors' approval within a few months. In the beginning, they simply refrain from the more complicated postures, such as the shoulder stand and the advanced twists. If you have never done yoga before, check with your doctor before starting, and make sure that your instructor is aware of your limitations. You may never get to the headstand—plenty of non-mastectomy people never do—but the benefits of even the most elementary yoga positions are unparalleled for flexibility, benefit to the inner organs, and a general sense of harmony and balance.

Even if you've never considered yourself as being athletic or physically active prior to the mastectomy, participation in non-competitive physical activity, such as swimming, dancing, and bicycle riding can awaken your body to potential you never realized was there.

There's an old expression that goes, "It doesn't matter if you win or lose—it's how you play the game." I'd like to alter that expression: "It doesn't matter if you win or lose or how you play the game—it's what you're doing for your entire body awareness that counts."

17
Sex

Although it is in the area of sexuality that the emotional implications of the loss of a breast are so traumatic, it is also the one aspect of a mastectomy that is glossed over so glibly by the mastectomy mystique. This is the area where the prosthesis cannot be expected to function in its role of "successfully fooling the world."

There is no question that this is the area where certain women will feel more threatened than others. No one can deny that it is the younger, single woman—either never married, divorced, or widowed—who will feel that the loss of a breast will either nullify or considerably reduce her chances of establishing a total, loving relationship. To imply that a married woman will not experience anxiety in this area would be to imply that intimate relationships between husband and wife are of no consequence, and a gross disservice. It has been found, however, that among couples whose marriage has been based on a sturdy foundation of mutual trust, support, and devotion, the shared experience of a mastectomy can create an even deeper bond of understanding between husband and wife which will, of course, ultimately find expression in their most intimate relations.

This is hardly to imply that the beginning will not be difficult either in an established marriage, other established relationship, or one that begins following the mastectomy. Granted, most mastectomy patients are bombarded with literature advising immediate resumption of sexual activity. The woman who wonders when she will be able to get off the hospital bed only has an added emotional burden upon reading this advice. For the woman, married or otherwise, who has regarded sex as a total body experience, this helpful hint can be interpreted as downright cruel. There is a basic need for the wounded animal to retreat. If a woman is able to tell her partner she would rather wait until sexual intimacy can, once again, resume its fullest meaning, it can, in itself, create a bond between the couple that none of the technical manuals on sex can approach—the bond of mutual understanding.

"Will he consider me repulsive?" is the uppermost question in the mind of the woman who has just undergone a mastectomy. Actually, this question should be rephrased as, "Do I consider myself repulsive?" There are few of us who have not been horrified at the first sight of the wound. When we, ourselves, are still in a state of shock at the loss, any man's protests that the loss of a breast doesn't matter to him will only be interpreted by us as pity on his part, if not a downright lie.

But it is in the area of sexuality that we will come to the realization that *the most important relationship in our lives is our relationship to our own bodies.* And there is nothing as effective as a balanced routine of sensible exercise, proper diet, and tender, loving care of our own bodies to make us aware of our full potential, both as sexual beings and as human beings. A heightened body awareness enables us to regard our total bodies as instruments of sexuality. There is no question that many women regard their bodies as being "dissected" into parts for different purposes—the digestive system for eating, eyes for seeing, legs for walking, and breasts and reproductive organs for sexual activity. These women, unfortunately, are cheating themselves out of one of the most meaningful aspects of human existence.

Our popular culture and mass media have contributed heavily to the myth that breasts are representative of sexuality, and even have tried to sell the idea that sexuality is virtually confined to breasts. Sadly, many women have not cultivated their entire bodies as expressions of sexuality. The woman who has undergone a mastectomy is in a unique position to gain an awareness of her total body as the fullest expression of love. The loss of a breast can also awaken us to the awareness of parts of our bodies that had previously been dormant.

As I have said before, the most essential step in enabling us to appreciate our "new" bodies is an awareness of our own grace and motion. Dancing for yourself as part of your exercise routine and catching glimpses of yourself in full-length mirrors will go a long -way in introducing you to your new body, and, consequently, your new self. If you're not yet ready to face your own scrutiny in a full-length mirror, try to break yourself in slowly by having the room slightly darkened.

In the beginning, there will be a tendency to hide in the presence of husbands or lovers. If you can discuss this openly with your partner, you and he have gone a long way in establishing what could be a deeper intimacy than you've known before. Some of the larger, looser, opaque nightgowns can help you over this hurdle. As your body acceptance increases, you will undoubtedly want to look into the more feminine nightgowns described in chapter 14.

I have heard stories of women who only make love while wearing a brassiere and prothesis. Personally, I can only regard this as I do such items as imitation breasts to be worn under lingerie—namely, perverse and obscene. Once again, I stress that if a woman feels she will never be able to reconcile herself to the visual fact of the mastectomy, she would be wise to seek consultation with her surgeon about the feasibility of an implant (see chapter 12).

Sexuality is probably the prime area where women—non-mastectomy as well as post-mastectomy—discover an unexpected plus as a result of a complete body program. As you discover your newly awakening body, sex will take on a new meaning in your life, above and beyond the physical act. Although much has been said and written about the awakening of an adolescent girl to changes in her body, much less has been said and written about the reawakening of the mature woman to a newly discovered body. And yet, it is the reawakened woman who has reason to rejoice. She is reaping the fruits of her own efforts. As your image of yourself changes, your partner's image of you will change accordingly. So will his appreciation of you and, perhaps even more important, his appreciation of himself and his own sexuality.

The foregoing may sound like well and good advice for the woman who has had an established partner prior to the mastectomy. What about the woman who had not been seriously involved with a man just prior to the surgery? Or the woman whose relationship with a man ended or became rocky following the surgery? So many younger, single post-mastectomy women have said, "I dread meeting new men and having to tell them about the mastectomy." Unfortunately, and inaccurately, these women feel that the mastectomy may create an obstacle to any lasting future relationship. The problem that these women are unable to foresee is that there are certain men who will be attracted to a woman *because* of the mastectomy—and such men are best avoided. This would be the type of insecure man with very low self-esteem who feels less threatened when a woman is dependent on him. They are the Casanova equivalents of the emotional vultures who thrive on catastrophe. Women in a weakened emotional state, no matter what the reason, unfortunately become easy prey for this man.

The soothing-syrup faction of the mastectomy mystique is quick to force-feed us with "happily ever after" tales of women who have met, become involved with, and married men following their mastectomies. This soap-opera approach vehemently denies the fact that any man could possibly have second thoughts about becoming involved with a woman who has had a mastectomy. A fool's paradise does not make a fitting habitat for any woman who has undergone a mastectomy. The truth of the matter is that there are men who are reluctant to embark on any involvement which carries responsibility. They are usually whining hypochondriacs who expect to be pampered by women. They are emotional grabbers who don't perform too well in the "giving" depart-ment—probably because they don't have very much to give. In addition to their other charms, they are bound to be, if I may use the vernacular, "lousy in bed." And as your own sexuality unfolds, you will automatically reject any potential partner who does not meet your standards.

The question still remains, "But how do I tell a man I've had a mastectomy?" The only answer I can give is, "It will tell itself at the right moment." To live in dread of making a dramatic an-nouncement will only add to your anxieties. As you become more accepting of the experience and as your body image improves, you will reach the point where you regard the mastectomy as one of the main character-building experiences of your entire life.

No one can deny that the so-called sexual revolution will have an impact on the younger post-mastectomy woman. Attitudes toward casual sex will have to be reexamined by the post-mastectomy woman (as they are being reexamined by the non-mastectomy woman). I hasten to point out that men who regard casual sex as an acceptable life-style are not going to be deterred by a mastectomy when they are interested in adding another attractive women to their "conquests." I cannot advise using the expression, "But I've had a mastectomy," as a deterrent to unwanted advances. A firm, polite (or not so polite) "No, thank you" is far more effective. Most younger post-mastectomy women have found that their fears of not being able to attract desirable men have been largely un-founded—while the problem of getting rid of undesirable men was largely unforeseen!

It is true that many women, following *any* traumatic experience in any area of their lives, can undergo feelings of unworthiness and consequent dependency which can, in turn, lead to frenzied, unsatisfying sexual relationships. This falls into the same category as heavy drinking or drug dependency, as the underlying problems are the same—it is merely the symptoms that change. In this case, a woman should not hesitate to seek qualified help (see chapter 9).

Aside from the emotional stakes, which are high for any woman where casual sex is concerned, there are unromantic realities that must be faced even more openly by a post-mastectomy woman. And most of those unromantic realities fall under the general heading of venereal disease, a category in which new strains are constantly being added to the time-honored classics, syphilis and gonorrhea. If a woman has relations with more than one partner who, in all probability, may have considerably more than one partner himself, she is well advised by more than one doctor to keep a supply of condoms on hand, over and above her approved contraceptive method, and make sure they are used for their intended purpose.

Options on contraception are more limited for the post-mastectomy woman than for the average woman. Most breast surgeons ban the pill entirely. The IUD (intrauterine device) is not contraindicated because of a mastectomy, but the wide range of problems it has caused is placing it under closer medical scrutiny. Foams and contraceptive gels used alone have a low reliability rating. In any case, the question of contraceptive methods is one that will have to meet the approval of your surgeon as well as your gynecologist. Surgical sterilization is an effective but extreme contraceptive measure and should be considered reservedly, especially by the woman who has had a mastectomy.

Sexuality is only one area where post-mastectomy women have found improvement in their lives, especially when they had anticipated disappointment. Total body awareness leads to a more complete sense of self. It is in this total relationship to one's self in all aspects that we find the basis of total relationships to those we love.

18
Family and Social Relationships

For several months after our mastectomies, most of our relationships with family, friends, and co-workers will be with people who have known us prior to the surgery. During the immediate postoperative period, we are not inclined to travel or enter situations that would bring us into contact with many new people.

But even with the people we've known for many years, subtle changes can come about in our relationships. It is in the area of social relationships that post-mastectomy women can be divided into two categories: the woman who has an established family life, husband, and children; and the younger, single woman, either never married, widowed, or divorced, who has hopes of forming a lasting relationship with a man. It is this latter group that has been rather callously neglected. Certainly, many women have met and married men following their mastectomies. Others have had their mastectomies prior to marriage, but during an engagement or other period when a relationship had already been established.

But for the woman who meets men following the mastectomy, the question "How do I tell him?" seems to reach gargantuan proportions. There is no pat answer to this question. As we, ourselves, begin to integrate the mastectomy into our total life experience, the question loses some of its obsessional quality. However, the younger woman who is convinced that her mastectomy automatically seriously diminishes her chances for forming a lasting relationship with a man has problems deeply rooted in her self-image, and she would be wise to seek some form of emotional therapy (see chapter 9).

For the single woman, the social problems are more than "What will he think?" Most younger, single women with active social lives travel, become house guests, and take part in dance or exercise classes where changing clothes is necessary. Questions like "Suppose the scar shows?" "Suppose they see me flat on one side?" "Do I have to wear the prosthesis *all* the time?" "Suppose I go on vacation and have to share a room with a woman I don't know?" are among the questions that pop up after the immediate fears and anxieties have been dealt with.

There is no one answer for every woman for every situation. In the beginning when we are still in the process of reconciling ourselves to the change, we are bound to be more aware, more self-conscious, and more touchy about it. Reassuring platitudes such as, "Oh, don't be silly, no one will notice, and if they do, they won't care, anyway," tend to aggravate rather than alleviate the problem. However, I think I can say in full confidence that *as we become reconciled to the fact, the fear of reactions from others will diminish in proportion.* Therefore, the question is not, "Shall I change clothes in a dressing room?" but, rather, "Have I yet reached the point where I can comfortably change clothes in a dressing room?"

For the woman who is the slightest bit edgy about the idea of being seen in a bra, I can only say, "Don't get yourself into a dressing room situation until you are ready to handle it." For dance and exercise classes, you can always wear slacks or a skirt over a leotard to class. If you're going to a store to try on dresses, the built-up lace slip illustrated on page 125 will make you feel comfortable. If you are going to try on a bathing suit or other sportswear, tell the saleswoman you would rather go into the dressing room alone but will ask for her help when you need it. (At this point, you might ask her for her name, as well.)

For a single woman, these questions will also come up when you are a house guest. Do you have to get into the prosthesis and bra before appearing at the breakfast table? The nightgown illustrated on page 124 minimizes the lack of symmetry. Especially if you've gotten into the habit of walking around at home without your prosthesis and bra, you might not think twice about appearing at the breakfast table in just the gown. But if you feel it might create any awkwardness when you are visiting, call your hostess aside and discuss it with her beforehand. Many women can accept the intellectual facts of mastectomy far sooner than they can accept the visual facts. I was fortunate during my first house-guest visit. Having become quite anxious that the twelve-year-old son of my host and hostess might see me without the prosthesis, I mentioned this anxiety to my hostess. Eleanor answered me with, "I've told Rick about your operation, and I'm so glad you're here. The more casual you are about it, the less he will worry if I should ever have to have a mastectomy." Eleanor probably deserved more credit in the matter than I did, but it should be mentioned that one of my aunts burst into tears when she saw me in "casual attire."

As far as sharing a room with a stranger is concerned, I can only say, play it by ear. When I told one roommate that she might see me "flat on one side," she answered very calmly, "Several of my friends have had mastectomies." With others, I made it a point to get undressed in the bathroom and wear the sleeping bra.

The nightgown that I have referred to above and which is illustrated on page 124 is actually loungewear rather than sleepwear. For softer, more feminine moments, I prefer "braless grace" to any sort of a padded nightgown. Flowing lines in a crepe nightgown or negligee, as far as I'm concerned, do more for classic femininity than any of the substitutes. However, this is an individual preference. In my own case, there came a day when, looking in the mirror, I decided to stop looking at the scar and start looking at the way my body moved. For me, one positive outcome of my mastectomy was that I became aware of inner grace rather than geometric surfaces.

For the woman with a husband and family, especially if the children are younger, the question of whether or not to be seen without the prosthesis is no longer one of occasional vacations or weekend visits with friends—it is an everyday question, and one of deep concern, especially in the beginning. As with the single woman, the first factor to consider is your own comfort. If you discuss this with your husband, it could clear the air rather than turn into an "underground" problem. Remember, the entire family will have to adjust to the change at first. If your husband honestly tells you that he prefers seeing you as he has been accustomed to, it will be.easier all around. Later, as you become reconciled to the reality, so will those around you. A loose housecoat or bathrobe, preferably gathered at the neckline, will provide graceful lines as well as comfort. In telling younger children about the operation, simply to say, "Mommy was in the hospital but she's fine now," and feel compelled to rush into the prosthesis and bra in the morning, can only create tension with which the children are unable to cope. If you tell them, in simple terms, what was done, and add that sometimes at home you will not appear the same as when you are fully dressed, you will go a long way toward creating a relaxed, harmonious atmosphere in your home.

The deepest change in your relationships is not going to be based on whether or not anyone sees you without the prosthesis. Women, especially, tend to regard us with a combination of fascination and fear: If it happened to you it could happen to them. We get used to frantic phone calls beginning with, "My cousin thinks she found a lump and she wants to know if you had a lump," or "The doctor told my sister she'd have to go for a mammogram. Is she going to have to have a mastectomy?" Unwittingly, we have had the label of expert pinned on us, and the wisest thing we could do is unpin it at the earliest opportunity. We have to learn to tell friends and relatives, patiently and calmly, that every case is different, and the top priority of the cousin or sister in question is to get to a qualified doctor as soon as possible. We also get bombarded with "My friend is seeing Dr. X and he said. . . . Is he any good?" Once again, refer your friend to the nearest detection clinic or comprehensive cancer center (listed in Appendix B) or the county medical society for a referral. You may be accused of sounding unsympathetic or uncaring, but, here again, calmness and patience are necessary. Explain that your best intentions are no substitute for qualified medical care. In fairness, you might point out that the cousin in question has a statistically high chance that a mastectomy will not be necessary, but it is essential that she see a qualified doctor. I refuse to give anyone guarantees that she will not have to have a mastectomy—I had too many guarantees given to me!

Dealing with friends of friends or cousins of neighbors is one thing. Dealing with close women family members is something else entirely. Our sisters and daughters are higher breast cancer risks than those of non-mastectomy women, and we have a serious responsibility to advise them to seek qualified care, and to mention this fact to their gynecologists or other physicians. Even our cousins should be advised of this. Especially if any of them is using the contraceptive pill, she will want to discuss it with her gynecologist.

Dr. Philip Strax, in his book, *Early Detection: Breast Cancer is Curable*, states the following:

> . . . if a woman has a mother or sister with breast cancer, her chances of developing the disease are increased from her usual odds of 1 in 15 to 1 in 10. However, she should have periodic breast examinations using the best methods available in her community.*

No one wants to be an alarmist, but this is one area where silence is *not* golden.

Recently, a problem has come up in social relationships following a mastectomy, especially in the case of the younger, sophisticated woman. The problem is the word *lumpectomy*. The woman who has undergone a mastectomy is not immune to comments from self-styled experts to the effect that her mastectomy was unnecessary; a lumpectomy would have been just as effective. Occasionally a few comments may be thrown in about a woman being the victim of her own naive ignorance as well as of a sadistic, mercenary doctor. Actually, serious consideration of the lumpectomy is far more dangerous to the pre-biopsy woman than it is to the post-mastectomy woman. A brief summary of the lumpectomy legend follows:

In 1973, George Crile, Jr., M.D., emeritus consultant in surgery at the Cleveland Clinic, published a book entitled *What Women Should Know About the Breast Cancer Controversy* (Macmillan). In this book Dr. Crile set forth his belief that there were cases in which "lesser surgery" could bring about the same results as radical surgery. In 1972, a patient of Dr. Crile's, Mrs. Rosamond Campion, wrote a book called *The Invisible Worm* (Macmillan), in which she described the success of her lumpectomy, performed by Dr. Crile. Mrs. Campion, whose professional specialty was fashion writing, was hailed on television and the press as the expert on treatment of breast cancer, and the expression "lesser surgery" became synonymous with "lumpectomy." Furthermore, Crile's name became associated with the lumpectomy. Although Dr. Crile

*Philip Strax, M.D. *Early Detection: Breast Cancer is Curable* (New York: Harper & Row, 1974) p. 27.

did advocate the lumpectomy in certain cases, I understand from reliable medical sources that he never has publicly announced the change in his stand. In fairness to Dr. Crile, it must be stated that he *never* advocated the lumpectomy as a viable alternative to radical mastectomy. "I do not recommend lumpectomy," he wrote in *What Women Should Know about the Breast Cancer Controversy.* "The minimal effective operation is partial mastectomy."*

However, the association stuck, and Dr Crile's alleged blanket endorsement of the lumpectomy is still righteously quoted by self-styled experts who seem never to have bothered to read his book. After her brief whirlwind of publicity, Mrs. Campion seems to have disappeared from the scene.

For those who seek the opinion of qualified experts, I am fortunate in being able to share the results of my discussion with Dr. Henry P. Leis, Jr., clinical professor of surgery and chief of the Breast Service at New York Medical College.

Dr. Leis is a leading advocate of "the surgery necessary as indicated by the individual case." Many people visualize the lumpectomy as being the removal of a lump, similar to the removal of a surface wart or mole. Actually, a lumpectomy usually involves removal of anywhere from one-quarter to one-third of the breast. What every woman needs to know about the lumpectomy is that it is not regarded as adequate treatment where a malignancy has been found. Factions of women's groups are still blissfully unaware that the lumpectomy as adequate treatment for breast cancer has been rejected by its founding father; nor was it ever common knowledge that among the ten-year survival figures reported in lumpectomy "success" stories, further surgery and accompanying treatment was necessary in close to half the cases reported.

Another pet theory of some groups is that a woman should have a choice of treatment, even if her surgeon disapproves of that particular method. "Find another doctor!" is the battle cry of those who think that a surgeon's interpretation of the Hippocratic oath includes acceding to nonnegotiable demands on the part of a patient.** What is likely to occur when a qualified doctor is

---

*George Crile, Jr., M.D. *What Every Woman Should Know about the Breast Cancer Controversy* (New York: Macmillan Publishing Co., Inc., 1973) p. 18.

**Ms.* magazine, September 1973, p.66.

commanded to perform any inadequate treatment is that the doctor himself will advise the patient to find another doctor. This advice will be given, not with a fist pounded on the desk, but spoken quietly, in the hope that the woman will seek the opinion of more than one ethical practitioner.

Most of us become quite irked when, shortly after the mastectomy, we're told how "lucky" we are. We don't feel exactly "lucky" in the prison of those bandages! It is only when a post-mastectomy woman has the opportunity of having a conference with a surgeon of Dr. Leis's caliber, and after receiving the complete picture on the results of the lumpectomy, that she is then fully able to understand just how lucky she is for having made her choice—the choice of a qualified, ethical practitioner!

Another war cry is that which states that mastectomies continue to be performed because of the male-dominated medical profession.

> Next, there is the malevolent influence of a male-dominated medical profession, specifically in surgery, reinforced by decades of discrimination against women by admission offices in medical schools, which has perpetuated the medical masculinity to the present. *

This opinion, however, does not include the feelings of many of the competent, ethical women doctors whose dedication to the medical profession has done so much to save the lives of women everywhere.

One such unsung heroine is Dr. Ruth E. Synder, whose professional involvement in the battle against breast cancer dates back to 1939. Working with mammography techniques, Dr. Synder has made a major contribution to the early detection, which is resulting in more and more women joining the 95-percent ten-year survival category. Dr. Synder believes that the strongest argument against the lumpectomy is a recently completed study on mastectomy specimens done at Memorial Hospital in New York City. After sampling all quadrants and axillary nodes of over 200 cases, Dr. Paul P. Rosen, associate attending pathologist, who

---

* Rose Kushner, *Breast Cancer: A Personal History and an Investigative Report*, Harcourt, Brace Jovanovich. New York & London, 1975, p. 316, from the chapter, "Male Chauvinism, Sex and Breast Cancer."

instigated the study, discovered that 62 percent would have had residual cancer, had only a lumpectomy been performed.

There is still another reason why Dr. Snyder is so respected in her stand on adequate treatment. She is not the only woman doctor who has willfully agreed to the extent of surgery necessary in both of her own mastectomies!

Another problem that exists for some post-mastectomy women that the masses tend to gloss over is the one of job prejudice. Although most working women have found their employers to be not only understanding but also eager and willing to make a post-mastectomy woman's return to work as comfortable as possible, cases of job prejudices have been reported, especially if a woman is seeking a new job following surgery or has been out of the job market for some time. As in the case of every form of prejudice, it is the outcome of ignorance. Probably the greatest unknown fact about cancer is that it is so often curable. This is not so with most other major diseases. Thanks to early detection and improved treatment, the cure rate is growing constantly. However, the hysteria lingers on. Another deep fear is that of contagion. Any sane, thinking person will realize that if cancer were contagious the entire world would have been stricken and the human race would have become extinct sometime around 5000 B.C.

Fortunately, responsible leaders of industry are investigating the matter and making their findings known throughout industry and government. The Metropolitan Life Insurance Company prepared a detailed report entitled, *The Employment of Persons with a History of Treatment for Cancer*, covering the years 1957 to 1972. I would like to quote from the section of that report entitled, "Observations and Conclusions":

> We conclude that the selective hiring of persons who have been treated for cancer, in positions for which they are physically qualified, is a sound industrial practice.*

It is not only in the area of employment that we will encounter prejudice as a result of having had a mastectomy. It can and does happen in ordinary social situations as well. The fear of "catching"

*George M. Wheatley, M.D., William R. Cunnick, M.D., Barbara P. Wright, M.D., and Donald van Keuren, *The Employment of Persons with a History of Treatment for Cancer; Cancer.* vol. 33, no. 2, February 1974, pp. 441–445.

any disease is probably most pronounced among hypochon-driacs—themselves often sufferers of a variety of mental and emotional disorders for which, as yet, medical science has not been able to offer any adequate treatment. Although they've often been made the butt of cruel, thoughtless jokes, they are seriously disturbed people who often paralyze themselves into inaction with worry. Most of them are unable to cope with even a visit to the dentist—how can they be expected to cope with any illness that would require clear thinking?

To realize that we've been avoided by anyone because we've had a mastectomy is not a pleasant thing to face. If we give the matter a little more thought, though, we will probably understand that the people who avoid us because of the mastectomy are probably the same people we would tend to avoid—whether or not we have had mastectomies.

There is no question that you will encounter changed attitudes in some people as a result of the mastectomy. Probably most im-portant and most beneficial of all, as a result of inner growth and development, your attitude toward yourself will undergo changes, and you will make the shift in your self-image from "Does this person accept me?" to "Do I want this person for a friend?"

It's a nice feeling. And it usually leads to improved family and social relationships.

19
Cultivating Enlightened Selfishness

Most of us, on hearing the word *selfish*, are quick to answer, "Oh, but I'm not like that," usually with a slightly self-righteous tone of voice. We still equate selfishness with greed, arrogance, insolence, and a total lack of consideration for others.

In this chapter, I'm talking about another kind of self-ishness—enlightened selfishness—in which we become aware that our top priority is *us*. It is only when we become aware of our inner selves and the shocking realization of the extent that we have been neglecting that inner self that we can begin to understand that enlightened selfishness is the first step toward equally enlightened consideration of others. Dr. Erich Fromm, in his classic, *The Art of Loving*, prefers to use the term *self-love*, and this is what he has to say:

> If an individual is able to love productively, he loves himself too; if he can love *only* others, he cannot love at all.*

Fortunately, we are living in an era in which we are reevaluating selfishness. For decades, anyone who ever wanted to be alone for any length of time was called introverted or antisocial, if not clearly neurotic. Most of us feel that even when we are alone, we have to be doing something productive—preferably productive

*Erich Fromm, *The Art of Loving* (New York: Harper & Row, 1956) p.50.

for others. How many of us have ever taken time out just to get to know ourselves?

The idea of being alone, or even planning to be alone, can be frightening to many people. Even more startling is the idea of creating an atmosphere of ease and relaxation simply for themselves. It is only recently that planning for time alone has become respectable.

Following a mastectomy, well-meaning friends and relatives feel compelled to distract us constantly. They are terrified that, left to our own resources, we will have a tendency to "start thinking" or "become morbid." We soon feel that a conspiracy is under way to prevent us from making contact with ourselves, as though our deepest feelings constituted an enemy.

The mastectomy itself was traumatic on many levels. The surrounding complications, worries, petty details, readjustment to everyday living, anxiety, and hysteria on the part of those around us, in addition to our own, have taken their toll. There is no one more entitled to peace and relaxation than we are. We need time to get it together, to reach that center around which is the basis of our own individuality and which, too often, has been overlooked in a misguided attempt to be considerate of others. The stress we have been through can only be described as inhuman. There is no love anyone could give us that can take the place of love of ourselves.

This enlightened selfishness is essential to our total functioning as human beings. Our love and respect for our deepest, innermost selves is the basis of our love and respect for others. Self-sacrificing martyrdom is the lowest form of bullying. Our prime responsibility is to ourselves—on every level.

Transcendental meditation, or TM, recognizes the need for every individual to get to his or her "center." TM, which, in its beginnings, seemed like just one more fad of the counterculture, has subsequently gained the respect and backing of leading medical researchers and practitioners. Its effectiveness in reducing strain and tension has been scientifically tested and proven. However, some people are beginning to become suspicious of some of the more blatantly commercial aspects of TM, especially its claims to cure the world of all its ills and the fact that it is being merchandised like one more household cleaning product.

Because of TM's popularity, the market is being flooded with books on the subject. Two of the best are *TM—Discovering Inner*

Energy and Overcoming Stress by Harold H. Bloomfield, M.D., Michael Peter Cain, and Dennis T. Jaffe, and *The TM Book* by Denise Denniston and Peter McWilliams. These two books explain TM—they do *not* teach you how to meditate. TM is simply not a do-it-yourself project, and the two-dollar meditation centers that flourish in large cities are to be avoided. If you want information about an approved TM center in your area, write to the International Meditation Society at 1015 Gayley Avenue, Los Angeles, California 90024, or at 59 West 46th Street, New York, New York 10036.

For you, enlightened selfishness may take the form of creating a luxury environment for yourself right in your own home. I discovered environment records. These include actual recordings of birds, forest sounds, rolling surf, thunderstorms, and gentle rain in a pine forest, among other natural sounds. One of my favorites is called "Tintinnabulation," a record of bell sounds that is difficult to describe. These records are not listened to as music is listened to. They have a relaxing effect of which the listener is virtually unaware. They are the most wonderful sounds I know for just getting in touch with yourself. If they are not available at a local record store, contact Syntonic Research, Inc., 175 Fifth Avenue, New York, New York 10010, and ask for their order form.

Enlightened selfishness takes some getting used to. You will probably feel more self-conscious in the beginning than you did at your first dance. We *are* our own severest critics. I eventually made myself a dressing gown just to be worn for my own luxury time (no brassiere and prosthesis underneath—*yippee!*). Did you ever think of having candlelight just for yourself? Dancing with your own shadow? Dressing up for a masquerade and just for a few moments becoming a great lady of a bygone era?

The expression *lady of leisure* conjures up in our minds visions of lazy, idle, parasitic women who go from club luncheon to fashion show to cocktail lounge, desperately trying to escape their own frenzied boredom. The woman who schedules leisure for herself is in a very different category. We are maintaining a balance in our lives that will make us more productive in our active lives—on the job, running a home, and being with others. To cheat yourself of enlightened selfishness means cheating those around you of a calm, composed, relaxed woman—wife, lover, friend, mother, or co-worker.

As you get to know yourself better and get used to your own company, you will discover inner resources that you never dreamed were there. You are alone with your fantasies and your imagination. Maybe it's time for you to step back for a change and let your fantasies take over. You can even start projects that are just for you. There is an indescribable joy in discovering an obscure author and reading just for your own enjoyment—*not* because you have to turn in a term paper. I personally "discovered" the great Indian poet, statesman, and philosopher, Rabindranath Tagore, during my own luxury time. (The world had discovered him seventy years before.) I cannot help quoting from one of my favorite Tagore poems, "Fruit-Gathering":

> Not for me is the love that knows no restraint, but like the foaming wine that having burst its vessel in a moment would run to waste.
> Send me the love which is cool and pure like your rain that blesses the thirsty earth and fills the homely earthen jars.
> Send me the love that would soak down into the centre of being, and from there would spread like the unseen sap through the branching tree of life, giving birth to fruits and flowers.
> Send me the love that keeps the heart still with the fulness of peace.*

In earlier cultures women were brought up and educated to develop their inner selves. An appreciation of music, art, and poetry were considered basic attributes of a gentlewoman. In the fast-paced, stressful living of the twentieth century, we would be wise to borrow a heritage from the past and resurrect graciousness, which some of us tend to regard as buried forever, like pressed flowers in a book.

If you had been forced to forego a vacation because of your surgery, this would be a good time to think of vacation plans again, even a type of vacation you had never considered before. If the financial aspect of the surgery created a hardship for you (as it did for me), you will be thinking about budget. As a result of my own

---

*Reprinted with permission of Macmillan Publishing Co., Inc., from *Collected Poems and Plays*, *Fruit-Gathering* #LXIII by *Rabindranath Tagore*. Copyright © 1916 by Macmillan Publishing Co., Inc.; copyright renewed 1944 by Rabindranath Tagore.

surgery I discovered mini-vacations: weekends spent differently from the way I usually live—in a large city. I have discovered farm vacations and ashrams, where members of the ashram (something like a commune) accept paying guests. As on the farms that accept paying guests, we are welcome to pitch in with the work if we so desire; otherwise, we are free to indulge in what I like to call "creative doing nothing." I have spent some very luxurious weekends for between $25 and $40.

The book *Farm, Ranch & Countryside Guide* lists 500 places that accept guests throughout the country. Accommodations are simple, but the rooms are clean and the food is wholesome and frequently homegrown. The book is available in some bookstores for $4. It can be ordered from Farm & Ranch Vacations, Inc., 36 East 57th Street, New York, New York 10022. Include $.50 postage for book rate or $1.00 for first class mail.

If you live on a farm yourself, a farm vacation would only be a busman's holiday. The important thing on any vacation is a change from your usual routine. Have you ever thought of spending a weekend at a hotel in a large city? You don't have to make the rounds of theaters and nightclubs. A leisurely walk through the shops, streets, and museums of an unfamiliar city can provide the change of pace and atmosphere you need. And if your family includes small children, breakfast in bed for you and your husband could become an added luxury.

Enlightened selfishness can mean different things to different women. If you love animals but don't find it practical to own a cat or dog, you can always find a willing friend or neighbor to lend you one. There are a few precautions to watch out for, though. Kittens, especially, should have been declawed before you start playing with them. There's rarely a biting problem with adult dogs, but puppies have a habit of nipping playfully, so keep the operative arm away from them. If you plan on walking a big dog on a leash, check on the dog's pulling habits first. Even though you will be holding the leash with the nonoperative arm, a sudden pull from a frisky dog could give you a jolt and you might have to use both hands. Even if you're walking a puppy on a leash, use the nonoperative arm.

Your form of luxury activity could mean going to the library every week and taking out an art book. Suppose you enjoy a type of film that your husband or friends find boring. It could be part of your selfishness program to see these films yourself. Even meeting a friend for coffee in a coffee shop with atmosphere could give you that sense of tender, loving care that we all need. The extra dime is worth it!

As you devote more time to developing your inner self, you will discover an "inner garden" that is beginning to bloom. It will be as though a veil has been lifted from your senses. Everyday sights and sounds will take on a new meaning. Even watching trees when a storm is approaching can become an involving experience. I live near a river that is banked by trees, and one of my favorite pastimes is watching the trees do a "ballet" before a storm.

You will soon discover that the luxuries you give yourself can never be matched by any gifts or flattery that anyone may offer you. Enlightened selfishness means enlightened self-discovery. It is this inner awakening and awareness that will give your womanhood a new dimension— a dimension undreamed of and unrealized prior to your mastectomy.

20
Vultures of the Living

"Quackery," according to Voltaire, "was born when the first knave met the first fool."

Voltaire made that statement in the eighteenth century. Today it would be a gross oversimplification to categorize every proponent of useless and often harmful "cures" for cancer as an out-and-out knave, just as it would be to classify every desperate relative of a cancer patient as a fool. Tragically, there have been some accredited physicians and scientists whose zeal and honorable but misguided intentions have propagated as much harm as the full-fledged charlatan, the latter perhaps often a grade-school dropout who has given himself or herself the honorary title of doctor. Equally tragically, many an educated, culturally enlightened person, who would smirk superciliously upon hearing of an "ignorant" person going to a witch doctor to have a hex removed, has fallen victim to the white-coated practitioner whose glib, pseudoscientific jargon promises the secret treatment that the medical Mafia has been trying to suppress.

Shifty-eyed moral vermin or misguided, once-respected physician, let us meet a few of them in these pages, as a precaution against ever meeting them in their offices or self-accredited "treatment centers." Among the "lettered" men and women who insist upon being addressed as doctor we find the following:

D.C.—Doctor of Chiropractic
D.P.M.—Doctor of Physical Medicine
N.D.—Doctor of Naturopathy
Ph.N.—Philosopher of Naturopathy
M.N.—Master of Naturopathy
Ph.C.—Philosopher of Chiropractic
D.N.T.—?
L.P.T.—?
T.G.—?

In the case of the last three, the meaning of these letters remains a complete mystery to the legal and medical professions. If the practitioners themselves know what they stand for, they're not about to divulge any trade secrets. Most of the above have received their professional training through "accredited" diploma mills, usually through correspondence courses.

The miracle cures generally fall into one of three basic categories, with each "doctor" issuing dire warnings against the use of a competitor's gadget, diet, enema technique, vitamin, or drug. These categories are (1) mechanical devices or machinery; (2) diet regimens either as specific cancer cures and cure-alls for *all* diseases or as general, all-purpose diets that prevent and cure every illness; and (3) drugs or "vitamins"—legal or otherwise. Following is a brief summary of each of these types of treatment:

Devices or Machinery

The zinc-lined pine box, called the orgone energy accumulator, is probably the best known. Herein lies the tragic story of a once-respected physician and colleague of Sigmund Freud named Wilhelm Reich, who was declared insane in his later years and died while serving a prison term, having been convicted of prescribing the orgone box as a cure for cancer. Like so many magic formulas, the orgone box was prescribed as a cure for a number of disorders and gained popularity among the misguided intellectual elite during the 1950s when psychoanalysis spawned fanaticism among its followers. Most purchasers of the orgone box used it in the (probably disappointed) hopes of improving sexual performance. Other less dramatic but equally ineffective devices include diathermy machines and electric juice extractors, usually sold in conjunction with diet cures. Rental or sale of some of this equipment can cost $1,000 or more.

Diet Regimes

"Natural" diets, "natural" treatment, "natural" vitamins, "doctors" of naturopathy, and "philosophers" of naturopathy have combined forces in recent years to give a grim new meaning to the time-honored medical expression, "Death due to *natural* causes."

There are probably more miraculous cures attributed to diets than any other form of illegal and ineffective treatment. These are carried as far as setting up of health farms or treatment centers to see that the diet is carried out according to directions. Emphasis is put on the word *natural*—no drugs or surgery. Of course, warnings are issued in abundance against the use of a competitor's "natural miracle" or "Miracle X." Frequent enemas are usually part of the routine.

Among the more prominent failures are the grape diet, uncooked fruits and vegetables only, uncooked vegetables that ripen above ground only, prohibition against all milk, egg, meat, and fish products, raw vegetables in conjunction with milk and honey, and coffee enemas in conjunction with injections of liver extract. Needless to say, each self-styled savior of mankind claims that his natural method is the only natural method, all other natural methods being unnatural.

Besides the specific cure diets, there are also the food faddists (calling themselves world-famous nutritionists) who preach their gospel (mostly through books in health food stores) guaranteeing perfect health in every area, as well as promises of prevention of every bodily disorder from dandruff to cancer and heart disease, while simultaneously improving sexual performance. One of the most recent diet fads promising both prevention and cure was the Zen macrobiotic or brown rice diet, supposedly based on the wisdom and philosophy of the Orientals (who, incidentally, have preferred white rice since the beginning of recorded history). This diet gained popularity among the counterculture college students during the sixties. Fortunately, few were able to stay on it long enough for it to do any irreversible harm. The Zen diet distinguished itself not only by its inability to cure any illness, but by its ability to kill previously healthy young people who followed it to the grain. It was written up in detail in the September 1971 issue of *Ladies Home Journal* by Dr. Frederick J. Stare, chairman of the Department of Nutrition, Harvard University, under the title "The Diet That's Killing Our Kids." An autopsy report following the death of a twenty-two-year-old woman who had remained on the diet for nine months reported "emaciation due to starvation."* (Her weight had dropped from 130 to 70 pounds.)

Drugs and Vaccines

These include animal cells, sera of various human and animal tissues, and enzymes with names like anticancer lipase enzymes. Two drugs in particular, krebiozen and laetrile, have received the support of various "health foundations" as well as individual practitioners. Both having been declared illegal in this country, a flourishing black market has grown in Mexico and parts of Europe, where cancer clinics abound. Laetrile alone has claimed fully half the share of the $2 billion illegal cancer cure industry. Many so-called health foundations, usually incorporated as nonprofit educational organizations, have been fighting to make laetrile available legally (claiming, as usual, that the "medical Mafia" was suppressing laetrile) and passing it off as vitamin B-17. The FDA declared that there was no such vitamin—it was simply a drug.

The July 21, 1975, *New York Times* featured a front-page story describing the results of four of the nation's leading cancer clinics having investigated laetrile and finding it to be totally useless in the treatment of cancer. Thorough investigation did, however, make one startling discovery that the promoters (or pushers) of laetrile either considered too trivial to mention or were too incompetent to discover. It was capable of causing cyanide poisoning. Laetrile had been made available as a vitamin, selling through health food stores under the names of Bee Seventeen and Aprikern. On April 18, 1975, an injunction was brought against General Research

*"Jury Rules Death by Diet," *A.M.A. News*, March 14, 1966.

Laboratories, Inc., of Van Nuys, California, against the sale and shipment of these two products. *

One of the most flourishing "health foundations," International Association of Cancer Victims and Friends (IACVF), was founded in 1964 by a Mrs. Cecile Hoffman, who attributed her "cure" of breast cancer to the use of laetrile. She died of metastic cancer in 1969.

There are two subjects on which there seems to be general agreement in the cancer quackery fraternity: (1) that there is absolutely no validity to anyone's miracle cure except that of the particular quack who is talking (or writing) and; (2) the use of the word *natural*, be it food, drug, or enema. However, not all the natural cures are as prosaic as a grape or a raw carrot (whose overconsumption can cause severe vitamin A toxicity). Among the more exotic natural treatments we have had over the years are cobwebs saturated with arsenic powder to "draw out" the cancer; the Jivaro Head Shrinking Compound (all natural ingredients, of course, a secret remedy given to a self-proclaimed "doctor" Ferguson as a result of his friendship with Tangamasha, chief medicine man of the Kenguimis); maggots; mushroom therapy; mud and mud products (although I have not been able to determine whether this latter is eaten, applied externally, or taken by enema).

It is not merely the twentieth-century version of the snake-oil-selling quack that creates one of the most serious deterrents to the effective treatment and often genuine cure of cancer. Books, some of them by reputable publishers, others by dubious publishing companies, play their part as well. Authors range from medical doctors to psychic healers to philosophers of naturopathy. Many of these books include cancer as merely one of the illnesses that will immeditely succumb to the author's spectacular discovery. The "blanket remedy" books invariably offer improved sexual performance. One book, offering molasses as the sure cure to all ills known to mankind, recommends douching with molasses as a cure

*Findings of Fact and Conclusions of Law, *United States of America v. General Research Laboratories, Inc.*, United States District Court, Central District of California, April 18, 1975, No. CV 73-2917-MML.

for uterine cancer.* In many cases, it could prove enlightening to check on the publisher's credentials as well as the author's.

One such book was written by a Max Gerson, who received his M.D. legitimately and was the founder of the Gerson Treatment—raw fruits and vegetables prepared in the juice extractor sold only by him in conjunction with injections of liver extract and coffee enemas. His book, *A Cancer Therapy,* was published by Dura Books, Inc. Preliminary research into Dura Books disclosed the following coincidental data: Officers included Mrs. Margaret Gerson (widow of Dr. Gerson, who died in 1959) as president; vice presidents and treasurer included Mmes. Johanna Oberlander, Charlotte R. Straus, and Gertrude Selten, all née Gerson, daughters of the kindly old doctor.

Freedom of the press, unfortunately, grants the same freedom to the irresponsible as it does to the responsible. As difficult as it is to get a book removed from the market, postal authorities have been successful in taking action against a book called *How to Cure Cancer in Two Months* by a Dr. Fairweather (actually, a Ph.D. in a totally unrelated field).

Why do people go to quacks? Sheer desperation is the prime motivation. Ignorance runs a close second. The word *cancer* still carries a terror totally unconnected with reality. How do these charlatans find their prey? What is the modus operandi of this species of moral vermin?

Unfortunately, infiltration of hospital waiting rooms and speaking to distraught patients or relatives is high on the approved list of techniques. One of the most heartbreaking examples of this method that has come to light in recent years is the case of a California couple whose eight-year-old daughter was brought to the University of California Medical Center for treatment to remove a cancerous growth in the child's eye. Removal of the eye, the parents were told, might save the child's life.

In the waiting room, a woman spoke with the child's parents and told them how a chiropractor "cured" her son of brain cancer without surgery. (What she was doing in the waiting room of an

---

*Cyril Scott, *Crude Black Molasses: Nature's Wonder Food*, Athene Publishing Co. Ltd., London, 1968, p. 15.

accredited hospital when a chiropractor had cured her son is a question that had evidently not occurred to the frantic parents.) In desperation, the child's parents removed her from the hospital's care and took her to the chiropractor, whose treatment included vitamins, unidentified pills, enemas, and special exercise. Needless to say, the tumor continued to grow, and when the parents realized the worthlessness of the treatment, they brought her back to the hospital. It was, of course, too late, and the child died shortly afterward. An autopsy report stated that the child's life might have been saved, and this became one of the all too few instances where the chiropractor was tried, convicted of second-degree murder, and sentenced to prison.*

Most quacks do not get to jail, though. They merely set up their clinics in other states, often becoming millionaires in the process. They usually cause quite a few deaths before the law can catch up with them, and even then, interstate law is fairly weak when it comes to nabbing a quack who has left the state. Medical quackery is a lucrative business—worth $2 billion a year.** And the more terrifying the name of the disease, the more terrified people will become, eager, anxious, and desperate to grasp at any straw in the wind.

It is not only individuals who propagate dangerously incompetent theories and treatment of cancer. Organizations such as the International Association of Cancer Victims and Friends (already mentioned), the Cancer Control Society, the Committee for Freedom of Choice in Cancer Therapy, the National Health Federation all play their part. Some of them are offshoots of previously existing organizations who have branched off due to internal squabbling. Some of them have political rather than medical aims, such as legalizing currently illegal drugs and treatment.

Probably the strongest ally of unproven or ineffective treatment against cancer is the mass media. A film star or other celebrity endorsing a "miracle cancer cure" on a TV talk show will draw an audience response second only to an "expert" offering unconventional sex practices as a cure for disturbed marriages. Gossip

---

*Marvin Phillips, the chiropractor, was tried, convicted of second degree murder, and sentenced to jail in the State of California in 1961. From *Unproven Methods of Cancer Management: Cancer Quackery*. American Cancer Society, New York, N.Y.

**The Fatal Choice: Cancer Quackery*, Charlotte Isler, R.N., Senior Nursing Editor, *RN Magazine*, September 1974.

publications will offer a miracle cancer cure to boost newsstand sales as readily as they will a report of friction in a Hollywood romance. The so-called health advice magazines are especially interested in unproven treatment regimes in addition to the hundreds of books and mass circulation magazines that regularly present false but favorable information regarding doubtful "discoveries" in the treatment of cancer.

These discoveries have not remained undiscovered by the American Cancer Society, which maintains a special division devoted to Unproven Methods of Cancer Management. A voluminous file on all aspects of worthless cancer remedies and devices has been accumulated. This material is made available to doctors, science writers, news editors, and other interested individuals. The society also publishes a booklet, *Unproven Methods of Cancer Management,* which contains reprints on individual worthless cancer remedies. It is available on request from the American Cancer Society, Inc., 219 East 42nd Street, New York, New York 10017.

If anyone, well-intentioned or otherwise, should approach you with glowing reports of "a new secret discovery that absolutely cures cancer," probably the most beneficial action you could take for yourself and your fellow human beings would be to check out the practitioner with your county or state medical society, the American Cancer Society, or your state health department. If someone suggests that you seek a particular treatment that has received the blessing of a nationally beloved stand-up comedian, you might want to check whether or not it has received the same blessing from your nearest Comprehensive Cancer Center (see Appendix B).

21
Womanhood Awakened

There is no set timetable for it. No one knows exactly when it will happen, nor can anyone predict exactly *how* it will happen. Like the life dormant within the seed, changes have been taking place subtly and imperceptibly. From wondering when you would be able to sleep in your usual position, you begin to wonder when you began sleeping in your usual position. From dread at facing the scar, you begin to wonder why no one ever told you the scar would heal so evenly and smoothly.

Others may have noticed and remarked on the changes in you before you, yourself, became aware of them. But suddenly one day you become aware of your awakened inner self. It could happen while looking into a full-length mirror and seeing the grace with which your body moves. It will come as something of a shock to realize that the flat side of your chest is part of your uniqueness. It could happen when you are walking along a wooded country lane and suddenly realize that you are one with all living things. Whether you live alone or are responsible for a large family, you will have discovered that your prime responsibility is to your inner self. You will have found time for your secluded moments—time out to become one with your deepest womanhood.

To attempt to deny the trauma of the mastectomy itself would be the equivalent of denying ourselves. It was through the shock, horror, and nightmare that we were able to reach the source of our inner strength. People who have lived through tragedy and up-heaval—be it war, the loss of a loved one, or a catastrophic ill-ness—have been known throughout history to develop an added dimension to their lives. If we are lucky, we are able to disdain the cloying sentimentality that too often accompanies loss and suf-fering.

We will never ask for, nor will we be given, citations, trophies, or medals for what we have experienced. Let's leave them to the hypochondriacs. The undefinable strength and confidence that results from having conquered a formidable enemy is ours. At first glance, it may seem that the disease itself was the formidable enemy we conquered. Probing on a deeper level, we gain insight to the fact that it was the dread we conquered—the nameless, in-describably paralyzing terror that inevitably surrounds a dread disease.

As we had to cope with changed attitudes on the part of those around us immediately following surgery, so will we have to cope with changed attitudes when we are fully recovered. Those who were eager to offer pity may not be so eager to offer ad-miration—especially if it is tinged with envy. A woman who has developed outer attractiveness as a result of having developed inner strength and beauty may find herself the target of resentment by women who feel that they are less attractive than she. Chronic complainers will feel threatened by a woman who has overcome serious obstacles in her adjustment to life.

Inner changes will inevitably manifest themselves in outer changes. Some friendships may cool as a result of this change, but they will unquestionably be replaced by deeper, more lasting ones. Our values have changed as well. We, ourselves, seek charac-teristics in people that we had not sought out before. We may even tend to regard our own pre-mastectomy way of life as having been shallow. We develop an inner pride in ourselves that is not to be confused with surface vanity. We tend to develop admiration for those who have overcome other obstacles. We are in a better position to offer human understanding as a basic component of our relationships than we were prior to the mastectomy.

We no longer take our bodies for granted. Many of us, since the mastectomy, have developed a style of our own in dress as well as bodily grace and carriage. Dependency feelings have been replaced by security feelings. As we have successfully coped with each step of the experience in all its ramifications—physical recovery, resuming responsibilities for the everyday details of our lives, the emotional turmoil—the attendant anxieties have diminished. By realizing that we will not live forever, we learn how to live. Questions such as "How will I ever. . . ?" have been answered with, "I did!"

Time spent alone, previously regarded as boredom, has taken on an entirely new meaning. Innermost feelings have become something to cherish rather than demons to be avoided and from which distractions must be sought constantly.

To say we will ever get over the loss of a breast is fallacious. There will always be moments when we look back upon the experience only to be faced with the unanswerable question, "Why?" And if we're honest with ourselves, this question will be followed by "Why me?" To speak of "accepting" the mastectomy is misleading. It would be more accurate to say we become acclimated to it. To pretend to negate the loss would be like trying to negate womanhood. I prefer to think that we have been compensated by a new dimension.

For so many of us, the mastectomy proved to be the turning point in our lives. It enabled us to emerge as more fully developed, fully integrated human beings. And when you realize that a totally functioning woman with one breast—or no breasts—can live a fuller, more deeply satisfying life than an incomplete woman with both breasts, you've won the entire battle!

Afterword

Those of us who have come through our mastectomies like to think of the experience as being completely behind us. Had we been prepared beforehand, we could have been spared weeks and possibly months of living nightmare. We can too easily forget that there are thousands of other women who are going through needless agony in anticipation of a possible mastectomy.

We have a responsibility to those women whom we have never met, just as we have a responsibility to the women in our lives who are close to us. Civic leaders, private industry, and the mass media must be made aware that the battle goes on not only for a cure for cancer but for enlightened awareness of the total needs of the pre-biopsy as well as the post-mastectomy woman. Individual surgeons and hospitals can issue printed matter for women entering the hospital. We are at least as entitled to a hot line for information, both preceding a biopsy and following a mastectomy, as alcoholics, drug addicts, unmarried pregnant women, and victims of venereal disease. Dance and exercise instructors should make every effort to structure their programs to the needs of *all* women. Medical people involved with breast cancer should cooperate with civic and industry leaders to enable the post-mastectomy patient to ease back into an active, meaningful life. Post-mastectomy women themselves will have to change their priorities from attitudes of shame to making others aware of our needs.

The non-mastectomy as well as the mastectomy woman has the right to full comprehension of catch phrases like *lumpectomy, lesser surgery,* and *freedom of choice.* Medical leaders will have to step forward in advising the lay public about complete facts and statistics in controversial issues rather than leaving the dissemination of this information to the sensationalist media. Although advances in detection and surgical procedure have resulted in cure rates undreamed of as recently as ten years ago, much remains to be done in battling the attitude of "I'd rather be dead than have only one breast"—an attitude that is, after all, deadlier than cancer itself.

APPENDIXES

Appendix A
Approved Cancer Detection Centers

These detection centers are sponsored by both the National Cancer Institute and the American Cancer Society. As there are usually waiting lists, appointments have to be made in advance. Suggested contribution is $25 for those who can afford it, but services are available at no cost to those who need them. This list is complete as of February 1976.

Note that these centers do not suggest or recommend any form of treatment. Should the X rays show anything doubtful, they suggest you report it to your doctor. If a specific doctor did not recommend you, these centers will guide you to a source in your area that will recommend a qualified physician.

EASTERN U.S.

Guttman Institute
200 Madison Avenue
New York, New York 10016
(212) 689-9797

University of Pittsburgh
    School of Medicine
3550 Terrace Street
Pittsburgh, Pennsylvania 15213
(412) 683-1620, ext. 461

College of Medicine and Dentistry
    of New Jersey
100 Bergen Street
Newark, New Jersey 07103
(201) 643-6431

Temple University
Albert Einstein Medical Center
York and Taber roads
Philadelphia, Pennsylvania 19141
(215) 455-8400

Rhode Island Hospital
Rhode Island Department
   of Health
Davis Street
Providence, Rhode Island 02908
(401) 277-5531

Wilmington Medical Center
P.O. Box 1668
Wilmington, Delaware 19899
(302) 428-2567

SOUTHERN U.S.

Emory University
Georgia Baptist Hospital
Atlanta, Georgia 30322
(404) 377-2472, ext. 303

Georgetown University
   Medical School
37th and O streets, N.W.
Washington, D.C. 20007
(202) 625-7125

Vanderbilt University
   School of Medicine
1161 21st Avenue, South
Nashville, Tennessee 37322
(615) 322-7311

University of Louisville
   School of Medicine
627 South Floyd Street
Louisville, Kentucky 40402
(502) 582-2111, ext. 510

St. Vincent's Medical Center
Barns Street and St. Johns Avenue
Jacksonville, Florida 32204
(904) 389-7751, ext. 8332

Duke University Medical Center
Durham, North Carolina 27710
(919) 684-4019

MIDWESTERN U.S.

University of Kansas
   Medical Center
Rainbow Boulevard at 39th Street
Kansas City, Kansas 66103
(913) 831-6101

Medical College of Wisconsin
561 North 15th Street
Milwaukee, Wisconsin 53233
(414) 258-2080

University of Cincinnati
   Medical Center
Eden and Bethesda avenues
Cincinnati, Ohio 45229
(513) 872-4396

Iowa Lutheran Hospital
716 Parnell Avenue
Des Moines, Iowa 50316
(515) 283-5205

University of Michigan
  Medical Center
1414 East Ann Street
Ann Arbor, Michigan 48104
(313) 764-1252

Ellis Fischel State Cancer Hospital
Business Loop
70th and Garth avenues
Columbia, Missouri 65201
(314) 433-3103, exts. 266, 260

WESTERN U.S.

University of Oklahoma
  Health Sciences Center
P.O. Box 26901
Oklahoma City, Oklahoma 73190
(405) 271-5134

Mountain States Tumor Institute
151 East Bannock
Boise, Idaho 83702
(208) 335-1780

Virginia Mason Research Center
911 Seneca Street
Seattle, Washington 98101
(206) 623-3700

Good Samaritan Hospital
  and Medical Center
1015 N.W. Twenty-second Avenue
Portland, Oregon 97201
(503) 228-6509

St. Joseph's Hospital
1919 LaBranch
Houston, Texas 77002
(713) 225-3131, ext. 269

Samuel Merritt Hospital
Hawthorne and Webster streets
Oakland, California 94609
(415) 451-8683

University of Arizona
  Arizona Medical Center
Tucson, Arizona 35732
(602) 882-7401

University of Southern California
University Park
Los Angeles, California 90007
(213) 225-3115, ext. 1677

Pacific Health Research
  Institute Inc.
Alexander Young Building
Suite 542
Hotel and Bishop streets
Honolulu, Hawaii 96813
(808) 531-8614

Appendix A

CANADA

While Canada does not have a breast cancer diagnostic center *per se*, the reader is referred to the following for advice:

National Cancer Institute of Canada
Dr. R. N. Taylor
Suite 401
77 Bloor Street W.
Toronto, Ontario
(416) 961-7223

Appendix B
Comprehensive Cancer Centers

The following list has been approved by the National Cancer Institute. They receive federal funds and are equipped to handle every phase of diagnosis and treatment. When calling or writing to them, state your specific purpose: a recommendation for a doctor, information about clinic services, where to get a mammogram, or whatever you need information on. This list is complete as of February 1976.

EASTERN U.S.

Memorial Sloan-Kettering Cancer
    Center
1275 York Avenue
New York, New York 10021
(212) TR 9-3000

Roswell Park Memorial Institute
Buffalo, New York 14203
(716) 845-3380

Sidney Farber Cancer Center
35 Binney Street
Boston, Massachusetts 02115
(617) 734-6000

Yale University Comprehensive
    Cancer Center
Yale University School of Medicine
333 Cedar Street
New Haven, Connecticut 06510
(203) 436-8213

The Fox Chase and University of
    Pennsylvania Cancer Center
Fox Chase Cancer Center
7701 Burholme Avenue
Philadelphia, Pennsylvania 19111
(215) FI 2-1000

University of Pennsylvania Cancer
  Center
School of Medicine
Room 264
Philadelphia, Pennsylvania 19174
(215) 243-7111

Johns Hopkins University
  Comprehensive Cancer Center
Johns Hopkins University
School of Medicine
Baltimore, Maryland 21205
(301) 955-5000

Georgetown University
Howard University Comprehensive
  Cancer Center
Vincent T. Lombardi
  Cancer Center
Georgetown University Hospital
Washington, D.C. 20007
(202) 625-0100

Howard University
College of Medicine
Washington, D.C. 20001
(202) 636-6270

SOUTHERN U.S.

University of Alabama
  Comprehensive Cancer Center;
  University of Alabama in
  Birmingham; University of
  Alabama Hospitals and Clinics
619 South 19th Street
Birmingham, Alabama 35233
(205) 934-3660

Duke University Comprehensive
  Cancer Center
Duke University Medical Center
Box 3814
Durham, North Carolina 27710
(919) 684-8111

Comprehensive Cancer Center for
  the State of Florida
University of Miami School of Medicine
Jackson Memorial Medical Center
P.O. Box 520875, Biscayne Annex
Miami, Florida 33152
(305) 325-6129

MIDWESTERN U.S.

Rush-Presbyterian-St. Lukes
  Hospital
1753 West Congress Parkway
Chicago, Illinois 60612
(312) 942-5395

Illinois Cancer Council
37 South Wabash
Chicago, Illinois 60610
(312) 346-9813

University of Chicago
   Cancer Center
University of Chicago
950 East 59th Street
Chicago, Illinois 60637
(312) 947-5777

Northwestern University
   Cancer Center
Northwestern University
School of Medicine
Chicago, Illinois 60611
(312) 649-8649

Mayo Foundation Cancer Center
Mayo Clinic
Rochester, Minnesota 55901
(507) 282-2511

Colorado Regional Cancer Center
1655 Lafayette Street
Suite 301
Denver, Colorado 80218
(303) 320-5921

WESTERN U.S.

The University of Texas
   System Cancer Center
M.D. Anderson Hospital and
   Tumor Institute
6723 Bertner Avenue
Houston, Texas 77025
(713) 792-2121

University of Southern California/
   LAC Cancer Center
University of Southern California
   School of Medicine
2025 Zonal Avenue
Los Angeles, California 90033
(213) 226-2008

Fred Hutchinson Cancer Center
   (affiliated with the University
   of Washington)
1102 Columbia Street
Seattle, Washington 98104
(206) 292-2931

University of Wisconsin
   Clinical Cancer Center
701C University Hospitals
1300 University Avenue
Madison, Wisconsin 53706
(608) 262-1626

Appendix B

CANADA

Note that the following facility is not under the auspices of the National Cancer Institute, which encompasses the United States only. However, it is recommended by the American Cancer Society.

National Cancer Institute
of Canada
Dr. R. N. Taylor
Suite 401,
77 Bloor Street W.
Toronto, Ontario, Canada
(416) 961-7223

Appendix C
Shopping Information

In the following lists, the companies with asterisks after their names have either a catalog or order sheet available, which you may request. As to the other companies, ask them for the names of stores in your area that carry their merchandise. You may want to request a specific item, such as a brassiere illustrated on a specific page, or a general category, such as bathing suits.

You will be able to order directly by mail from the companies with asterisks. The others will provide you with shopping information in your area.

*Temporary Brassieres and
Breast Forms*

Confidante
Berger Brothers Company
135 Derby Avenue
New Haven, Connecticut 06507

Jodee, Inc.
200 Madison Avenue
New York, New York 10016

Appendix C

Nightgowns

Empire State Mastectomy Salon*
1307 York Avenue
New York, New York 10021

Regenesis, Inc.*
18 East 53rd Street
New York, New York 10022

Jodee, Inc.
200 Madison Avenue
New York, New York 10016

Slips

Regenesis, Inc.*
18 East 53rd Street
New York, New York 10022

Wide-Sleeved Shirts

H. Kauffman & Sons Saddlery Co.*
139-141 East 24th Street
New York, New York 10010

Regenesis*
18 East 53rd Street
New York, New York 10022

Sew-In Pockets

Jodee, Inc.
200 Madison Avenue
New York, New York 10016

Bathing Suits
(Mastectomy Designed)

Sea Scamp
Camp International, Inc.
109 West Washington Street
Jackson, Michigan 49201

Jodee, Inc.
200 Madison Avenue
New York, New York 10016

*Write for mail order catalog or order sheet.

The following companies manufacture bathing suits not specifically designed for post-mastectomy women but suitable, nevertheless, in many cases.

Waterclothes
1411 Broadway
New York, New York 10018

Cole of California
1411 Broadway
New York, New York 10018

Danskin, Inc.
1114 Avenue of the Americas
New York, New York 10018

Peter Pan Swimwear
1407 Broadway
New York, New York 10018

Rose Marie Reid
1407 Broadway
New York, New York 10018

Roxanne Swim Suits
10 East 32nd Street
New York, New York 10016

Sandcastle
110 East 9th
Los Angeles, California 90015

Prostheses (*Indicates brassiere
manufacturers as well)

AIR-FILLED PLASTIC

Camp International, Inc.*
P.O. Box 89
Jackson, Michigan 49204

Confidante*
Berger Brothers Company
135 Derby Avenue
New Haven, Connecticut 06507

Restoration
P.O. Box 1541
Fairfield, Connecticut 06430

FOAM

Accentuette
Culver City, California

NUE'DE
Madelon Louden Co.
403 South Wall Street
Los Angeles, California 90013

Silveco Products, Inc.
2502 Milwaukee Avenue
Chicago, Illinois 60647

Appendix C

Camp International, Inc.*
P.O. Box 89
Jackson, Michigan 49204

Confidante*
Berger Brothers Company
135 Derby Avenue
New Haven, Connecticut 06507

Jodee, Inc.*
200 Madison Avenue
New York, New York 10016

SILICONE FILLED

ACTIVE
Stryker Corporation
Kalamazoo, Michigan 49001

Camp International, Inc.*
P.O. Box 89
Jackson, Michigan 49204

COMPANION*
Airway Surgical Co.
Erie Avenue
Cincinnati, Ohio 45209

CUSTOM MADE

MATCH MATE
Dr. Eugene L. Harris
1203 North Euclid
Anaheim, California 92801

PERFECT MATE
Ruth Merzon
233 West 77th Street
New York, New York 10024

Records/Tapes

Environmental Records
Syntonic Research, Inc.
175 Fifth Avenue
New York, New York 10010

Dance Instruction Tape Booklet
Ms. Dorothy Hill
Manhattan School of Dance
78 Fifth Avenue
New York, New York 10011

Suggested Reading

Bloomfield, Harold, M.D., Cain, Michael Peter, and Jaffe, Dennis T. *TM—Discovering Inner Energy and Overcoming Stress.* New York: Delacorte Press, 1975.

Denniston, Denise, and McWilliams, Peter. *The TM Book.* Allen Park, Michigan: Versemonger Press, 1975.

Fromm, Erich. *The Art of Loving.* New York: Harper & Row, 1956.

Hittleman, Richard. *Yoga Twenty-Eight Day Exercise Plan.* New York: Workman Publishing Company, Inc., 1969.

Kubler-Ross, Elizabeth, M.D. *On Death and Dying.* New York: Macmillan Publishing Company, Inc., 1969.

Strax, Philip, M.D. *Early Detection: Breast Cancer is Curable.* New York: Harper & Row, 1974.

Tagore, Rabindranath. *The Collected Poems and Plays of Rabindranath Tagore.* New York: Macmillan Publishing Company, Inc., 1913.

Farm, Ranch Countryside Guide. Farm & Ranch Vacations, Inc. New York: 1974.

Index

Additives, chemical, 73, 77
Aerosol spray products, 82
Air-filled plastic prostheses, 135, 187
Air-inflatable bra, 132
Airway all-Lycra bra, 133
Airway Companion bra, 133
Alcohol, drinking, 79
American Board of Plastic Surgery, 83–84
American Cancer Society, 83, 168, 169
American Hospital Association, 52
Anti-mastectomy sentiment, 71
Anxieties, 4, 5, 31–37, 44, 60, 149
  about the scar, 35–36
  of attractiveness to husband, 34
  and depression, 31–37
  pep talks and, 37
  sexual activity, 35
Aprikern (laetrile), 165–166
Art of Loving, The (Fromm), 156
Artemis, 91
Asanas, 91
Aura Groups, 61
Awareness. *See* Reawakening phase
Axillary lymph nodes, removal of, 9

Balance exercises, 39
Bathing suits, 116–122, 137
  and matching skirt, 120
  shopping for, 186–187
Bathtub mats, 19

Beauty care, 80–87
  cosmetic surgery, 83–84
  cosmetics, 81–83
  at home, 18–20
  silicone breast implants, 84–87
Beauty School of Bergen County, 20
Bederson, Barbara, 61
Bee Seventeen (laetrile), 165–166
Biopsy, 3, 67
Bloomfield, Harold H., 157–158
Body awareness:
  exercise and, 90–91
  sex and, 146
Brassiere, for temporary use, 12–13, 21
Breast Cancer: A Personal History and an Investigative Report (Kushner), 46, 153
Breast Service (New York Medical College), 152
Burkard, Kristine, 61

Cain, Michael Peter, 157–158
Camp Tres Secrete air-inflatable bra, 132
Campion, Rosamond, 151, 152
Cancer Control Society, 168
Cancer Detection Centers (U.S. and Canada), 177–180
Cancer Therapy, A (Gerson), 167
Chemotherapy, 53, 82
Chiropractors, 167–168

Index

Clenched fist syndrome, 44
Cleveland Clinic, 151
Clothes, 106–126
  for at home, 20–21
  hospital stay, 14, 16
  immediate needs, 110–113
  long-range needs, 113–116
  mail-order service for, 107, 112–113
  See also Prosthesis
Cole of California, 118
Collected Poems and Plays, Fruit-Gathering (Tagore), 159
Comaford, Carter M., 69–70
Committee for Freedom of Choice in Cancer Therapy 168
Comprehensive Cancer Centers (U.S. and Canada), 169, 181–184
Confidante (manufacturers), 13, 126
  Moulded Cup bra, seamless, Style No. 493, 21, 111, 132
Consumer Reports, 130
Contraception, 145–146
Cosmetic surgery, 83–84
Cosmetics, 81–83
County Medical Society, 83, 86
Crepe nightgown (or lounge gown), 124
Crile, George, Jr., 151–152
Crude Black Molasses: Nature's Wonder Food (Scott), 167
Cunnick, William R., 154
Custom-made prostheses, 135, 188

Dance classes, 139
Dancing, 143
Danskin bikini, 121
Death, fear of, 49–52
Deep-armhole shirt:
  dressing yourself in, 20
  for immediately following surgery, 16
Denniston, Denise, 158
Deodorant, use of, 81
Diathermy machines, 164
Diet, 54, 72–79
  drinking and, 79
  quackery, 164–165
  reducing plans, 74

  shopping for nutrition, 76–79
  supplements, 78
  weight reduction, 74–76
Dietz, J. Herbert, Jr., 21
Directory of Medical Specialists, 84
Divorce, 44
Doctors, resentment against, 33
Dolman sleeve, 114
Domestic problems (post-surgery), 23–26
Douching, 56
Downer, Carol, 55
Dritz Zipper Pull, 20

Early Detection: Breast Cancer Is Curable (Strax), 151
Elbow raise (exercise), 96–97
Empire State Mastectomy Salon, 14, 107, 110, 116, 126, 130
Employment of Persons with a History of Treatment for Cancer, The (Metropolitan Life Insurance Company), 154
ENCORE (Encouragement, Normalcy, Counseling, Opportunity, Reaching Out, Energies revived) program, 60–61, 89–90, 137
Environment phonograph records, 158
Euthanasia Education Council, 51, 52
Euthanasia Society, 49, 51
Evening gowns, 126
Exercise, 26, 39, 54, 81, 88–105
  body awareness and, 90–91
  doctor's approval for, 12, 88, 92
  in the hospital, 11–12
  instructions for, 92–105
    elbow raise, 96–97
    leg stretch, 102–103
    shifting weight, 100–102
    shoulder roll, 93–96
    torso stretch, 97–98
    waist roll, 99–100
    waist twist, 103–105
  meaning of, 88
  programs, 88–90
Extended radical mastectomy, 9–10

Facing the facts, 38–48
  ability for, 38–42
  fiction and, 43–48
    breast-oriented society, 45–46
    lumpectomy, 46
    psychiatry, 46
    same person you always were,
      44–45
    sex object myth, 46
    sexual relations, 45
    understanding another mastec-
      tomy woman, 45
    your husband, 44
Fad diets, 74
Family relationships, attitudes and,
  147–155
Farm, Ranch & Countryside Guide,
  160
Farm & Ranch Vacations, Inc., 160
Fatal Choice, The: Cancer Quackery
  (Isler), 168
Feminist Women's Health Center
  (Los Angeles), 55
Fibrefill breast pad, for temporary
  use, 12–13, 21
First Women's Bank (New York
  City), 50
Foam prostheses, 134, 187
Food and Drug Administration
  (FDA), 165
Freud, Sigmund, 163
Fromm, Erich, 156
"Frozen shoulder," preventing, 12

General Research Laboratories, Inc.,
  165–166
Gerson, Margaret, 167
Gerson, Max, 167
Gerson Treatment, 167
Goodyear, Clelia, 59, 60, 61
Guthrie, Randolph H., Jr., 83, 85,
  86
Guttman Institute, 6
Gynecological care, 54–57

Hair thinning, 82–83
Halsted radical, 36
Halter-top dresses, 125
Hart, Joyce, 110, 116, 130

Health clubs, 137–139
Health food stores, 76–77, 78
Hill, Dorothy, 90
Hippocratic oath, 152
Hirsch, Lolly, 55
Hittleman, Richard, 91
Hoffman, Cecile, 166
Hospital, resentment against, 33
Hospital gown, 14, 109
Housework, 24–26, 39
*How to Cure Cancer in Two
  Months* (Fairweather), 167
Hygiene, at home, 18–20
Hypochondria, 58

Imitation breast, 132
International Association of Cancer
  Victims and Friends
  (IACVF), 166, 168
International Meditation Society,
  158
Invisible Worm, The (Campion),
  151
Isler, Charlotte, 168
Isolation, feeling of, 4
IUD (intrauterine device), 145

Jaffe, Dennis T., 157–158
Jivaro Head Shrinking Compound,
  166
Job prejudice, 153
Jodee, 13, 126, 131
  bra and prosthesis, 134
  bra Style No. 500, 21, 111
  nightgown with pocket for pros-
    thesis, 123

Kauffman's (New York City), 112–
  113
"Keeping our cool" attitude, 41–42
Keuren, Donald van, 154
Kiss, Michaeline, 90
Kohut, Helen Glines, 88–89
Krebiozen, 165
Kubler-Ross, Elisabeth, 49–50
Kushner, Rose, 46, 153

Ladies Home Journal, 165

Index

Laetrile, 79, 165–166
Lasser, Terese, 5, 12, 88
Leg stretch, 102–103
Leis, Henry P., Jr., 152, 153
Leotards, 122
Lesion excision. See Partial mastectomy
Lingerie, 126
Liquid-filled prostheses, 135, 188
Lister, Joseph, 5
Living Will (Euthanasia Educational Council), 51, 52
Local excision. See Partial mastectomy
LoCurto, Camille S., 50
Lumpectomy, 6, 8
    attitudes toward, 151–154
Lymphatic glands, function of, 18, 54

McWilliams, Peter, 158
Makeup, experimenting with, 81–82
Manhattan School of Dance, 90
Manicure, 82
Mastectomy:
    categories of, 8–10
    facing the facts, 38–48
    fiction, 43–48
    first steps (process of rebuilding), 2–63
    number of operations, 47
    pre-biopsy needs, 3–7
    reawakening phase, 67–174
Medical Center of Princeton, 89
Meditation, 158
Megavitamin theory, 78
Memorial Hospital (New York City), 11–12, 83, 153
Metropolitan Life Insurance Company, 154
Minipoo (shampoo), 14
Modified radical mastectomy, 9
Monroe, Marilyn, 146
Mount Sinai Hospital (New York), 56
Ms., 152

National Health Federation, 168
Necklines, 116

New Women's Survival Sourcebook, The, 55
New York Medical College, 152
New York Times, The, 165
Nightgowns, 122–126, 149
    for hospital stay, 14, 109
    prices of, 110
    shopping for, 186
    with sleep puff, 108, 110
    when sleeping, 23
92nd Street YM–YWHA (New York City), 61

Oberlander, Johanna, 167
Organically grown foods, 77, 78
Orgone energy accumulator, 163

Pap test, 54–55
Partial mastectomy, 8–9
Patient's Bill of Rights (American Hospital Association), 52
Peter Pan (manufacturers), 118
Phillips, Marvin, 168
Phonograph records or tapes, shopping for, 188
Physical activity, participating in, 136–140
Plastic surgery, 9–10, 29, 83-87
    cosmetic, 83–84
    silicone breast implants, 84–87
Plastic Surgery Services (Memorial Hospital), 83, 86
Post-Mastectomy Rehabilitation Service (Memorial Hospital), 11–12
Pre-biopsy patient, needs of, 3–7
Primary chest muscles (pectoralis major), 9
Prosthesis, 127–135
    basic types of, 134–135
    comfort and appearance, 128
    construction of, 131
    cost of, 132
    decision for, 13
    doctor-approved, 130
    myths about, 127–128
    proper fit of, 130–132
    questions to ask the doctor, 128
    sex and, 141

shopping for, 187–188
and swimming, 130–131
washability of, 130
See also Clothes
Pssst (shampoo), 14
Psychiatrists, 46

Quackery, medical, 162–169
as a deterrent to effective treatment, 166–169
devices and machinery, 163–164
diet regimes, 164–165
drugs and vaccines, 165–166
practitioners of, 162–163
reason for, 167
TV shows and, 168–169
*Questions and Answers on Death
and Dying* (Kubler-Ross), 50

Radiation therapy, 53, 85
Radical mastectomy, 9
lumpectomy myth alternative to,
46
"Ratcatcher" shirt, 112
Reach to Recovery program, 5–6,
7, 12, 13, 34, 110, 111
philosophy of, 5–6
Reawakening phase, 67–174
awareness of life, 67–71
beauty care, 80–87
clothes, 106–126
diet, 72–79
enlightened selfishness, 156–161
exercise, 88–105
family and social relationships,
147–155
prosthesis, 127–135
quackery and, 162–169
sex, 141–146
sports and physical activity, 136–
140
womanhood, 170–172
Rebuilding process, first steps in,
2–63
anxiety and depression, 31–37
death fears and, 49–52
making a will, 50–52
facts, 38–48
and fiction, 43–48

at home, 17–30
body exercises, 26
clothing, 20–21
cooking, 25–26
domestic problems, 23–26
going to a job, 28
going on a vacation, 29–30
household work, 24
hygiene and beauty care, 18–
20
precautions to take, 17–18
questions to ask doctor, 17
resting, 21
sexual activity, 22–23
sleeping, 21–22
at the hospital, 8–16
arm exercises, 11–12
checklist for, 10
clothing, 14, 16
eating food, 10–11
getting out of bed, 11
immediate goals and needs, 12
and leaving, 15–16
occupational therapy, 14–15
prosthesis and brassiere, 12–13
psychological help, 58–63
related health matters, 53–57
gynecological care, 54–57
visits to doctor's office, 53–54
See also Reawakening phase
Reducing pills, 74
Regenesis (boutique), 14, 107, 126
slips, 125
wide-sleeved shirt by, 113
Reich, Wilhelm, 163
Resentments, 40
Rest and relaxation, 21, 54, 81
RN Magazine, 168
Rose Marie Reid (manufacturers),
118
Rosen, Paul P., 153–154
Rothman, Lorraine, 55

Sandcastle (manufacturers), 118
Saunas and steam rooms, 138–139
Scars, 29
anxiety about, 35–36
types of, 36
Schizophrenia, 78
Scott, Cyril, 167

Index

Sea Scamp bathing suit, 117
Secondary chest muscles (*pectoralis minor*), 9
Self-examination, method of, 53, 54
Selfishness, enlightened, 156–161
  meaning of, 156, 160–161
  by meditation, 157–158
  reevaluating, 156–157
  self-awareness and, 158–159
  vacations and weekends, 159–160
Self-pity, 40
Selten, Gertrude, 167
-Sew-in pockets, shopping for, 186
Sexual activity, 22–23, 141–146
  anxiety, 35
  in the beginning, 143
  and body awareness, 146
  casual relationships, 144–145
  contraception, 145–146
  fact and fiction about, 45
  prosthesis and, 141
Shampooing at home, 19
Shaving underarm, 81
Shifting weight (exercise), 100–102
Shopping:
  for bathing suits, 186–187
  list of companies, 185–188
  by mail order, 185
  for nutrition, 76–77
Shoulder roll (exercise), 93–96
Shower attachments, 19
Silicone breast implants, 9, 84–87
  cost of, 85
  "perfect match," 86
  procedure for, 85–86
  questions to ask the surgeon, 87
Silicone-filled prostheses, 135, 188
Simple mastectomy, 9
  with axillary lymph node dissection, 9
Skin cancer, 83
Skin grafting, 85
Sleeping comfort, 21–22
Sleeveless clothing, 115
Sleeves, 114, 115
Slepp, Adam, 20
Slippers, for hospital stay, 14
Slips, shopping for, 186
Smith, Cathy, 107
Social relationships, 147–155
  for the single woman, 147–149

for woman with husband and family, 149–151
Socializing, post-operation, 26–27
  morbid curiosity seekers and, 27
Sports, participating in, 136–140
Stage Hairdressers, 19–20
Stare, Frederick J., 165
Stiff upper lip attitude, 40
Straus, Charlotte R., 167
Strax, Philip, 6, 151
Suicide, 5
Sunlight, overexposure to, 83
Swedish massage, 138
Synder, Ruth E., 153–154
Syntonic Research, Inc., 158

Tagore, Rabindranath, 158–159
Terrycloth scuffs, 14
Torso stretch (exercise), 97–98
Tranquilizers, 79
Transcendental meditation (TM), 157–158
TM Book, The (Denniston and McWilliams), 158
TM—Discovering Inner Energy and Overcoming Stress (Bloomfield, Cain, and Jaffe), 157–158
Truppin, Michael, 56, 57

Underpants, 122
  for hospital stay, 14
United States of America v. General Research Laboratories, Inc., 166
U.S. Department of Health, 75
University of California Medical Center, 167–168
Unproven Methods of Cancer Management: Cancer Quackery (American Cancer Society), 168, 169
Uterine cancer, 56, 167

Vacation, 158–159
Veg-It (seasoning), 77–78
Vitamin A, 78, 166
Vitamin C, 79

Vitamin D, 78
Vitamin E, 79
Vitamin fads, 78–79

Waist roll (exercise), 98–100
Waist twist (exercise), 103–105
Waterclothes (manufacturers), 118, 119–120
Weight reduction, 74–76
Weight Watchers, 75
What Women Should Know about the Breast Cancer Controversy (Crile), 151, 152
Wheatley, George M., 154
Wide-sleeved shirts, shopping for, 186
Wigs, 82–83
Wills, 50–52
Womanhood, awakening of, 170–172

Women's movement, 6, 146
Wright, Barbara P., 154

X rays, 3

Yoga, 90, 139
Yoga for Health School, 90
Yoga Twenty-eight Day Exercise Plan (Hittleman), 91
Yogurt, 77
Young Women's Christian Association (YWCA), 60–61, 89–90, 137

Zen macrobiotic diet, 164–165
Zinc-lined pine box (orgone energy accumulator), 163
Zippers, 20